SHIPS OF THE
Victorian Navy

SHIPS OF THE
Victorian Navy

BY
CONRAD DIXON

Published in association with
THE SOCIETY FOR NAUTICAL RESEARCH

Ashford Press Publishing
Southampton
1987

Published by Ashford Press Publishing 1987
          1 Church Road
          Shedfield
          Hampshire
          SO3 2HW

in association with the Society of Nautical Research

British Library Cataloguing in Publication Data.

Dixon, Conrad
    Ships of the Victorian navy.
    1. Great Britain. *Royal Navy* — History
    2. Warships — Great Britain — History — 20th
    century
    I. Title
    623.8'25'0941   VA454

    ISBN 1-85253-033-2   Hardback
    ISBN 1-85253-024-3   Paperback

Printed in Spain by Mateu Cromo Madrid

CONTENTS

LIST OF ILLUSTRATIONS

PREFACE

Some years ago a publisher friend set aside two volumes of coloured prints of Victorian ships of the Royal Navy with the instruction that they be given to me after his death. At one time he had intended to reprint them himself, but he was overtaken by serious illness and unable to achieve his aim. The prints were by Fred Mitchell and there was a general introduction and comment by Francis Elgar, a naval architect who had been chief assistant to Edward James Reed, the controversial, argumentative but highly talented Chief Constructor of the Navy until 1870.

The Mitchell prints were the glory of these volumes and depicted the eloquence of that vanished age when seamen wore their jumpers tucked inside their trouser tops, sported straw hats in the tropics and often worked barefoot. Life was not easy for them. Ships had to be coaled every few weeks, there was no air-conditioning or refrigeration, hardly any mechanical aids. Tours of duty on foreign stations were measured in years, and naval discipline was almost as harsh as it had been in the age of sail.

In providing a new introduction and commentary on every ship, Conrad Dixon, a seasoned seaman and former Royal Marine officer, has drawn largely on the material contained in the 73 volumes of *The Mariner's Mirror* which embody the expertise and knowledge of past and present members of the Society for Nautical Research. He will be the first to admit that we all owe a great debt to early writers like Admiral George Ballard who served in many of the ships described here, and who lived through the transition from the wooden-hulled sailing ship to the steam-driven ironclad. What strikes one most on looking back through *The Mariner's Mirror* is that while rivalry was intense between Britain and France (for there was no great Russian or American fleets to balance the scale), there was little ship-to-ship action. Apart from episodes such as the bombardment of Alexandria and minor skirmishes in distant waters often involving the landing of marines and seamen, the guns were hardly ever fired in anger.

Our interest in these times is stimulated by the coming this year to Portsmouth of the restored battleship *Warrior*. She will join *Victory* at Portsmouth, and we will be able to compare the first of the iron battleships with perhaps the greatest of the last surviving wooden walls.

March 1987
Brian H. Dolley
Hon. Editor
The Mariner's Mirror

vii

Chapter 1

THE ENGINEERING REVOLUTION

The Victorian Navy was the product of an engineering revolution in the three areas of propulsion, fabric and weapons. The changes from sail to steam and wood to metal are central to the advances in design made in the reign, while the ships described in this book are, in one sense, specimens in a display cabinet showing the development of a species. The variety of the ships reflects the changing demands of empire, the threat from other great powers, notably France, the theories of naval architects, the machinations of politicians and, occasionally, the hard-won experience of seamen. The industrial revolution is technically complete when the young Queen Victoria comes to the throne, but it has hardly touched naval shipbuilding. Massive wooden walls, such as *Trafalgar*, are being built, but the technology is static. Large timber, the fruit of centuries of growth and careful planting, has become scarce with the heavy demands of the Napoleonic period, while a size limit has been reached where hogging and sagging stresses inhibit any increase in ship length. It is tempting to propound a hypothesis that had there been no engineering revolution, and plenty of tall trees, the age of cast iron guns and wooden hulls would have spilled over into the twentieth-century and either softened the impact, or even prevented the commencement, of two world wars.

The 38 years of relative peace prior to the outbreak of the Crimean War had seen only one major battle at sea – the annihilation of the Turkish fleet at Navarino by a combined British, French and Russian force. No aspect of new technology had been involved, and fifteen years later in the early 1840s the Admiralty remained fundamentally committed to wood and canvas. Most of Britain's warships were laid up in reserve for most of the time, and new construction was a leisurely business, spread over years, and concentrated at the Royal Dockyards at Chatham, Portsmouth, Devonport, Deptford, Woolwich, Pembroke and Sheerness. The steam paddler had been rising in importance in the commercial world, and the Admiralty was content at first to use the new device merely for pulling sailing warships in and out of harbour. From the orthodox naval point of view the steam-paddle ship was of limited utility. The fragile boxes and wheels took up most of the central part of a warship where broadside guns could best be deployed; engines could, and did, often fail whereas masts and sails were reliable except in a flat calm. There were other factors of a more tenuous kind. The steam engine was a smelly nuisance, its smoke blackening spars and canvas. The engineers did not fit into the hierarchy and might conceivably come to threaten the command structure by knowing more about moving the ship than the captain and his officers. The exposed machinery of a paddler could easily be put out of action by a well-aimed shot from an enemy. On the other hand, screw propulsion was a slightly more acceptable proposition. It was out of sight, the screw was not likely to be hit by enemy fire and the engines could be installed down in the bilges and below the waterline. In 1842 the matter was put to a decisive test.

Two ships, the *Alecto*, a paddler, and the *Rattler*, screw propelled, were lashed stern to stern for a tug-of-war contest. The issue was soon decided when *Rattler* dragged her opponent across the line with ease. It would be wrong to say that the lesson learned was applied at once, for the Admiralty continued down the cul-de-sac of paddle propulsion for a short time. The frigate *Penelope* was cut in half, lengthened by about 65 feet and fitted with a paddle engine. Other paddle frigates included the *Terrible* (nicknamed the *Black Sea Cat* in the Crimean conflict), but in evolutionary terms this was a dead end as the virtues of the screw propellor became widely appreciated. In particular, a stern-tube could be bored through the stern-post of a wooden hull without the necessity of rebuilding; the propellor itself could be lifted up and down in a well when the ship was under sail and the funnel, or funnels, could be lowered or raised. The order 'Up funnel, down screw' was coined to signify the transition from sailing to steaming, and the whole question of the appearance of a warship was crucial in moulding opinion. In order to understand fully the acceptability of the steam screw warship it is instructive to look at the lithographs of *Victory* and the *Duke of Wellington* in this book.

First, they are superficially very similar in appearance. *Victory* is, of course, the *beau idéal* of a wooden wall, a ship much prized by successive fleet commanders and a revered relic. She typifies the peak of naval greatness in about 1810 when over a thousand British ships of all types held the seas. This force was sufficient to blockade Europe, maintain an extensive overseas empire and fight any two other navies at the same time. She was armed with just over a hundred guns firing shot weighing from 12 to 32 pounds and two 68 pound carronades. The *Duke of Wellington* has 130 guns, the heaviest firing shot of 68 pounds weight. The real difference lies in performance. *Victory* could head through an arc of about 240° at about 6 knots; *Duke of Wellington*, with a steam engine driving a single screw propellor, could head through an arc of 360° at a speed of 10 knots. From this we may deduce that *Duke of Wellington* had the edge over *Victory* in offensive terms; can we say the same in the defensive mode?

Events in 1853 and 1855 proved the utility of armour. The so-called 'massacre' of Sinope in the former year describes the crushing defeat of the Turkish fleet at Sinope Roads in the Black Sea. The Russians were firing shells from rifled guns at unprotected wooden hulls equipped only with smooth-bore guns, and the result was that only one Turkish ship escaped out of thirteen engaged – and the escapee had an auxiliary steam engine. The other side of the coin was revealed two years later when Russian shore batteries at Kinburn near the estuary of the Dneiper engaged three French warships, the *Lavé*, *Dévastation* and *Tonnante*. The mastless Frenchmen lay only 800 yards offshore but the Russian gunners were in despair at making no impact on the enemy. After 3 hours of fruitless firing the Russians hoisted the white flag. The ships, wooden ships, had been plated with an iron armour of between 4 and 5 inches thickness so that even in a long engagement no serious hurt had been received, and only two men were killed. *Victory* and *Duke of Wellington* were unarmoured. They would both have been pounded to matchwood at Sinope, and been forced to withdraw at Kinburn.

The contest between guns and armour was highlighted by the American Civil War engagement between *Merrimac* and *Monitor*. The former was a Confederate Navy frigate of the conventional kind, but unconventionally protected by a sloping roof of railway iron. *Monitor* was a purpose-built turret ship plated with iron and sitting very low in the water. In the event, neither ship could do the other much harm, and the British Admiralty came to certain decisions about new construction. Experience in the Baltic and Black Sea, together with the deductions that could be made from the *Merrimac* and *Monitor* confrontation, meant that the armoured ship had an advantage over its unarmoured rival, while shell-firing guns could shatter wooden hulls. The first question to be answered was: what thickness of iron was needed to prevent penetration by the shot of a 68-pounder – the most powerful gun then in service – at a range of 200 yards? It was discovered by practical experiment that a plate of iron, 4½ inches thick and backed by teak, would resist the impact. The rule was then formulated that armoured warships should be built with 4½ inches of iron on 1½ feet of teak backing. At the same time, it was necessary to do something about ships still on the stocks, and *Royal Alfred* is the perfect example of a wooden ship to whom these criteria were hastily applied. The first new construction based on the four principles that a warship should be armoured, sea-going, powerfully-gunned and fast was that of *Warrior*, launched in 1860.

Many designs had been submitted, and many compromises made, to ensure that the ship was a success. She was now to be built wholly of iron, to be long – for speed is a function of length, to have the heaviest guns available, and to be armoured. She could not be armoured everywhere, and the eventual decision was to protect her gun battery, boiler, engines, magazines and shell-rooms. Her engines gave a speed of over 14 knots. *Warrior*, and her classmate *Black Prince*, were remarkable ships, but it will do no harm to point out a few deficiencies. Their great length made them hard to handle, and they could only fire broadsides. The rudder head and steering gear were unprotected, and there were two anachronistic features in the design. There was a wide frigate stern that added 50 tons of weight for the sake of tradition, while the graceful bow was a fraud that hid a blunt ram. Finally, the 4½ inches of plate over the central part of the hull was soon found to be unequal to the penetrating power of new guns.

At the end of the 1850s the Admiralty was still ambivalent about switching to breech-loading guns. The effect of rifled weapons in capable hands had been noted, but the Armstrong gun of 1858 was both rifled and a breech-loader, and the conventional wisdom was that a proper gas-tight breech block did not exist. As a result, many of the ships described in this book were initially armed with the rifled, but muzzle-loading, weapons in their early years, being converted to breech-loaders in the 1880s. Muzzle-loading had the effect of keeping barrels short, and thus restricting range and accuracy. William Armstrong's first guns were of wrought-iron, but he developed the technique of shrinking a wrought-iron jacket over a rifled steel tube. This steel tube was replaceable, and the guns had a much longer life. At the close of the period studied Armstrong's company had perfected a way of making guns that has lasted almost to the present day. A steel tube was bored from an ingot, and rifled so as to give the shell a twist as it left the barrel. Miles of tough steel wire were wound round the tube to form the body of the barrel, and metal rings were forged over that to keep it all together. The change to breech-loading was greatly facilitated by an unfortunate accident in 1879. One of *Thunderer's* guns blew up, and the verdict was one of double-loading. Double-loading, the ramming home of two lots of bags of explosives, or two projectiles, is possible with a muzzle-loader; it can't be done with a breech-loader where the shell is rammed home until the soft copper driving band at its base engages in the lands of the rifled barrel. The remaining space in the breech can only accept *one* charge of powder or cordite.

Chapter 2 deals with the changes that took place in the years 1862–82, and the emphasis will be on the shape and composition of the Royal Navy as dictated by national requirements, the theories and prejudices of designers and the practical application of the engineering revolution to warship design.

Chapter 2

DESIGNS AND DESIGNERS

In the 1860s and 1870s Britain was supremely confident of her position in the world. The first industrialised nation, she had an excellent infrastructure by way of railways, docks, factories and warehouses. Her civil servants were honest; Peel's police had a good grip on the classes predisposed to riot and disorder, and money was sound. A middle class governed on the principle of Buggins' Turn; the emotions stirred up by the French Revolution had cooled while Marx and Engels had yet to put across the concept of the class war. The franchise had been widened, and would be widened again when the Liberals brought the propertyless poor to the hustings. Colonies channelled their produce to the mother country, and Britons living abroad knew that, in the ultimate resort, a naval vessel would come and avenge wrongs and slights. The Royal Navy was seen as having three responsibilities. The consular aspect has just been referred to, and the other priorities were coast defence and the meeting of a hostile fleet on the high seas. This gives us the outline of three types of ships likely to be wanted. Colonial cruisers of medium size and great endurance to patrol the more distant parts of the world. Heavy guns in shallow-draught hulls for protecting the coasts. Fleets centred on battleships to fight the foreign foe. The principal candidate for the foreign foe was France; the chief danger areas for aggrieved subjects and businessmen were Africa, the Pacific and the Middle East.

In 1861 the emphasis was on capital ship construction, for in that year no less than eleven major warships were ordered. *Achilles* was a modification of *Warrior*, but the class comprising *Minotaur*, *Northumberland* and *Agincourt*, designed by Isaac Watts, were 400-footers with heavy guns and an inch more armour, *Hector* and *Valiant* were improved versions of *Defence*, while the five ships of the *Caledonia* class which included *Royal Alfred* were converted two-deckers with the 4½ inches of armour thought necessary to make them ironclad frigates. This surge in construction drew public attention to what had previously been the preserve of professionals, and the two principal theorists of the day were Edward James Reed, the Chief Constructor at the Admiralty in succession to Isaac Watts from 1863–70, and Captain Cowper Coles, a naval officer with a burning zeal for turret ships. Reed saw warships as broadside carriers with a small number of heavy guns carried in a battery amidships and protected by armour. An additional belt of armour was to protect the waterline, so that his approach was called the Belt and Battery System. The Coles concept was one of revolving turrets in a highly-protected ship with a low freeboard so as to minimise the effects of enemy fire. His thinking had been formed by his experiences during the Crimean War when he had supervised the building of a low-profile raft with a 32-pounder on it, and the *Monitor* experiment of the American Civil War.

In the beginning, the proposals of the Chief Constructor carried most weight. A forceful, not to say bad-tempered, individual, Reed was a brilliant designer and he had the sense to appreciate that improvemental change would cause the least trouble with naval officers, the Admiralty and the general public. The design for *Bellerophon* was his first following his appointment, and she was an all-iron ship, eighty feet shorter than *Warrior*, but carrying broadside guns that could penetrate the latter's armour at 2000 yards. *Bellerophon* had more armour and a complete double bottom to help maintain watertight integrity if the outer skin was pierced. *Hercules* and *Sultan* were improvements on *Bellerophon*, with more armour still and improved fields of fire. The division of opinion between Reed, who was basically a defensive designer, and the more aggressively-minded Coles was not absolute, for Reed could see that the turret had some advantages, but was not compatible with masts and spars. Ironically, when he was allowed to design a blue-water turret ship by the Board under the abrasive Controller, Spencer Robinson, he was forced to include a fo'c'sle and a full sailing rig that served to obstruct the workings of a revolving turret. At the same time the Admiralty was not entirely deaf to Cowper Coles' case, and an 1865 committee had looked at his designs and, while not approving every proposal, nevertheless thought that some aspects were worth pursuing. From this sprang two ships that are central to our understanding of the period. *Monarch* was an experimental, sea-going turret ship built with Admiralty blessing; *Captain* was built by Lairds of Birkenhead to Cowper Coles' modified designs with rather more grudging approval.

In a sense, both ships were flawed by the attentions and deficiencies of officialdom. Coles had intended that *Captain* should have a low profile, and his designed freeboard was 8 feet, 6 inches. However, he was ill when she was being built and through a miscalculation in the drawing office at Lairds the ship ended up with less than 7 feet of freeboard when fully loaded. Her metacentre was over 7 feet below the waterline. This might have been detected if the Admiralty had agreed to supervise the work on the ship, but the most that the government department would concede was that an overseer would check the *quality* of materials but not their *weight*. Coles must also bear some blame, as he had such confidence in the design that he equipped her with the tallest and heaviest masts in the fleet; masts that were stayed on the tripod system so as to keep down the reduction of arc of fire caused by shrouds being in the way. *Monarch* was a turret ship that could not fire forward or astern, and thus may be classified as merely an improved central battery design due to the obstruction caused by her fo'c'sle and rigging. In various tests between the two ships some conflicting claims were made. *Captain* was said to be faster under sail; *Monarch* faster under sail and steam together. There was no contest about stability. *Monarch* never exceeded 15° of roll in all her service; *Captain* had a calculated danger figure of 21°, and her loss was attributed at the court martial to the 'heave of the sea'. Reed resigned as Chief Constructor shortly afterwards, nominally to take up a post with Whitworth's, the engineers, but he admitted that the loss of *Captain* 'had its weight in all that happened'. Cowper Coles went down with his ship.

The Admiralty had fewer doubts and hesitations when they placed orders for shallow-draft, powerfully armed and armoured turret ships such as *Hotspur* and *Glatton*. The former was intended as a steam ram, with her powerful forward-facing gun designed to keep the enemy's head down as she steamed up to crush the foe underfoot. *Glatton* was a heavily-protected monitor, with *Devastation* following as a larger sea-going ship of the same type. *Dreadnought* was in the same tradition, and had the thickest complete belt of armour of any British warship. The reason seems to be that Reed, the defensive designer, had started the design when the ship was to be called *Fury*, while it had been finished off by his successor and brother-in-law, Nathaniel Barnaby, another defensive designer but one who lacked the spark of genius in Reed. Indeed, some academic commentators point to a decade of decline, or even a 'dark age', in the 1870s when Barnaby was following a policy of a 'fleet of samples' and leadership at the Admiralty was weak. This thesis can certainly be supported if we look at ships like *Inflexible*. She was a citadel ship designed by Barnaby to take enormous punishment, and her offset turrets and uncompromising appearance caught the public imagination. Was she efficient as a fighting machine? The verdict of history goes against her, for when tested at the bombardment of Alexandria three salient facts emerge. Her rate of fire was desperately slow; the great clouds of smoke from her guns prevented the fall of shot being readily observed, and the concussion smashed the upperworks and her boats. The case that Barnaby was inadequately supervised may also be supported if we look at the development of the colonial cruiser.

This is a shorthand term for vessels designated as frigates or corvettes that are heavily armed, but not armoured, and expected to do the work, as one writer has it, of an 'imperial gendarmerie'. Nathaniel Barnaby was an enthusiast for this type of vessel, for it fitted in with his 'Liberal' view that the work of the Navy was best accomplished by a number of small, cheap ships. *Inconstant*, one of Reed's designs, was an early prototype, but *Boadicea* is probably the first 'cruiser' in the proper sense. The Victorians put their colonial cruisers into three classes, first, second and third, and ships such as *Active* and *Volage*, technically corvettes, are splendid early examples of second-class cruisers; *Boadicea* and *Bacchante* first-class. In the lowest class comes *Comus*, launched in 1878. These vessels retained masts and sails to the end of their lives for coal depots were not always within range on colonial stations, while their bottoms were often sheathed in copper or zinc because there was limited access to dry docks. Some of them served for 4 years without attention below the waterline. The principal advantage was that an inexpensive peace-keeping force was always available for the protection of the British interest abroad, while the imperial representatives had small packets of sailors, marines and guns at hand for dealing with any petty tyrant, minor insurrection or banditry. The disadvantage was that these ships had been ordered piecemeal and had differing armaments, engines and sail wardrobes so that the supply side could only be attended to properly at a home dockyard. Surprising as it may seem nowadays, very few discussions took place at the Admiralty to establish classes of ships for particular purposes before the 1890s.

One of the characteristics of the period is that there were few opportunities for the live-testing of weapons or for revising gunnery techniques in battle conditions. At Kinburn the armoured ship had the edge over the shore batteries, and that situation of advantage was to be tested again at the bombardment of Alexandria in 1882. The causes of the conflict need not detain us long. There had been rioting in the city, and some Europeans had been killed. An Egyptian minister seemed to have had dictatorial ambitions, and the forts around Alexandria were being refurbished and their guns made ready. An ultimatum brought no results, and punitive action was decreed. The ships taking part were an interesting cross-section of the Royal Navy of the time. *Inflexible* was there, low in the water, heavily protected, massively armed. *Monarch*, the ship that had survived the storm that sank *Captain*, *Alexandra*, *Sultan* and *Temeraire*, *Superb* and *Invincible*. The tactics were elementary. Three of the major ships were to take up position close to the shore, and five would shoot from beyond the breakwater. Five gun vessels would stay out of range in the early stages until there was a chance to steam in and pound weakened positions. *Inflexible* was stationed at the outer end of Corvette Pass so that one turret could engage the Lighthouse Fort and the other the Oom-el-Kubebe Fort on the mainland. The *Temeraire* was to handle the Mex Forts with *Monarch* assisting and *Invincible* and *Penelope* further inshore. *Sultan*, *Superb* and *Alexandra* had as target the heavily-manned fortifications on the Ras-el-Tin peninsula.

The combination of weaponry was very mixed. *Alexandra*, *Monarch* and *Sultan* had, as main armament, 11-inch, 12-inch and 10-inch guns, respectively. *Alexandra* was the most successful of the battery ships, as she could fire forward as well as broadside. *Monarch's* turrets had no axial field of fire, while *Sultan* was basically a broadside ship, with two guns forward unprotected by armour. *Temeraire's* problem was that her aft gun could not be trained and fired on any bearing without damaging the bulkheads under the poop. The bombardment itself was a slow business, with ships taking all day to fire between 80 and 300 (in round figures) shells apiece. The Egyptian batteries were silenced, but the surprise of the day was the performance of the gun vessels, or rather one gun vessel, the *Condor*, under Lord Charles Beresford. Seeing that Fort Marabout at the western extremity of a line of fortifications was pouring heavy fire into *Invincible*, *Penelope* and *Monarch*, *Condor* steamed close inshore to get under the muzzles of the enemy and inflicted considerable damage at close range. When the wrecked forts were examined it was found that the relatively light shells of the gun vessel had done as much damage as the massive projectiles of the battleships. *Inflexible's* guns had used 450 pounds of powder at each discharge; the question that now arose was that perhaps this enormous force was unnecessary as much lighter guns were achieving the same degree of impact. Further analysis of the results left no room for complacency. Over half of the shells had either failed to burst, had burst prematurely or had split on impact. One unexploded shell was found in a magazine containing 400 tons of gunpowder. The armour had justified its expenditure, for only five men were killed. The gunnery record was unimpressive, and it transpired later that one significant contributory cause was the type of ammunition used. Most shells were of the Palliser armour-piercing type with a small bursting charge; what was needed for an attack on a land fortress was common shell with a heavy pushing effect to blow down walls and disable gunners.

A balanced fleet that gives value for money must contain more than just battleships, cruisers and coast defence vessels, and the Victorian Navy probably got best value from its smaller units. The usefulness of *Condor*, gun vessel, at Alexandria has already been shown, and the same may be said about the smaller gunboats which kept the peace and showed the flag on, say, the China station at very little cost. Sloops, such as *Wild Swan* and *Cruiser*, were available for anything from anti-slavery patrols to putting men on shore to fight war-lords or rebels. They were, in effect, fourth-class colonial cruisers. Sloops and other small ships often remained on station with a crew-change from home at the end of a commission, and here the troopers like *Orontes* or *Himalaya* had a part to play. Ships used for surveying could double as expedition vessels, while experimental vessels were found jobs that squared the accounts. *Iris*, for example, a cruiser in all but name, was for some years called, and used as, a despatch vessel. Sometimes, politicians acted hastily and did not get value for money. Years of indifference to naval needs under Disraeli was followed by a panic decision in 1878 to buy tonnage in a hurry during the Russian war scare. The result was *Neptune* – probably the least useful battleship ever acquired. In their defence, politicians and designers could point to the pressure of developing technology inhibiting the creation of a truly balanced fleet, and it is certainly true that a policy of homogenous classes of ships was not arrived at until two conditions were satisfied – they were the reaching of a technology plateau in about 1889, and the passing of the Naval Defence Act in the same year.

Finally, it is necessary to say something about a weapon that occupied the same significance in naval thinking as the nuclear device does today – the torpedo. Invented in 1867, the Whitehead torpedo caused a crisis of confidence among designers to which they responded in different ways. Preventive measures were tried in the form of torpedo nets, but the notion was soon put on the back burner as it was appreciated after the *Hotspur* trials that this type of defence system would only suffice for stationary ships. . . . Next, searchlights and quickfiring guns were tacked on to the upper decks of ironclads – the guns being of Nordenfeldt or Hotchkiss make, Gardners and Maxims. Torpedo carriages were fitted to many ships, and *Shah* actually fired a torpedo at *Huascar*, but to no good effect. Two classes of torpedo boats were developed. The larger class was able to keep the seas, and the type was later employed in both world wars. The small torpedo boat as depicted by Mitchell was carried by a mother-ship and hoisted in and out in the fashion of the more traditional launch or cutter. Naturally, torpedo boats were of more interest to nations that had few capital ships, but the first British boat, named *Lightning*, was built in 1877. Torpedo craft were painted black to deceive lookouts at night, and the antidote to them was not perfected until the 1890s when the Torpedo Boat Destroyer came into service. The sea-mine and the submarine are just over the horizon in 1882 when this commentary must come to an end, and it is only proper to finish with some prophetic words from Francis Elgar, the designer who first introduced Fred Mitchell's lithographs to the Victorian public. He notes that Germany, Italy, France and Russia are expanding their navies and broods over the torpedo menace. 'The ship,' he writes, 'is in greater peril of sudden and terrible disaster than ever . . . there are signs that armour on the sides of ships, to which they owe their distinctive position as Ironclads, is to be abandoned.' The capital ship is at this point both a manifestation of power in iron and steel, and the symbol of a new insecurity.

NOTES ON THE DATA

Length   is the length between perpendiculars to the nearest foot.

Tonnage   is displacement tonnage.

Guns   are described either by calibre (6-inch) or by weight of shot (64-pounder). The barrel and loading method is shown by:

                  ML Muzzle-loading

                  BL Breech-loading

                  SB Smooth Bore

                  R Rifled

so that, for example, MLR means that the gun is a muzzle-loader with a rifled barrel.

Horsepower is the nominal horsepower unless more closely defined.

Speed   is the mean top speed ascertained by averaging runs over a measured distance.

THE ILLUSTRATIONS

These are by William Frederick (known as Fred) Mitchell, who was born at Calshot Castle in 1845 and died at Ryde in 1914. He was a reclusive near deaf-mute who made his living by painting pictures of ships for naval officers. He had an arrangement with Griffin's Bookshop at No 2 The Hard, Portsmouth to take orders for this type of work, and the firm printed two volumes of *The Royal Navy in a Series of Illustrations* containing Mitchell's lithographs, which are reproduced in this book. The same shop sold Mitchell's prints for framing. A number of other pictures by him, many in watercolour, are preserved at the National Maritime Museum, Greenwich.

Chapter 3

SHIPS OF THE VICTORIAN NAVY

HMS ACTIVE

CORVETTE, LAUNCHED 1869, 270 FEET LONG, 3080 TONS

Armament	Designed to carry six 7-inch MLR guns and four 6-inch MLR guns. After 1880 fitted with ten 6-inch BL guns, two 6-inch guns and two 14-inch torpedo tubes.
Designer	Controller of the Navy.
Builder	Thames Shipbuilding Company, Blackwall.
Horsepower	4015 Indicated Horsepower.
Speed	15 knots; 12½ knots under canvas.
Scrapped	Sold out of the service in 1906.

A sister ship to *Volage*, *Active* was constructed of iron with an outer skin of oak and having copper sheathing below the waterline. Her design derived from that of *Inconstant*, with speed as a primary consideration. She did not enter service until 1873 when she went as the commodore's ship on the Cape of Good Hope and West African station.

Her crew served ashore in both the Ashanti and Zulu Wars, and one of them perished far inland at Isandhlwana in 1879. He was a signalman attached to an officer on Lord Milne's staff, and it is recorded that he fought to the last with a sword bayonet and his back to a wagon wheel until speared from behind by a Zulu assegai. Captain Fletcher Campbell of *Active* noted with some surprise that there was only one one serious defaulter during eight months of campaigning, and he was a thirsty stoker who could not resist sampling a bottle of brandy incautiously stowed in a stores wagon.

Paid off in 1879, *Active* was rearmed and refitted, but had no role to play until 1885 when she was selected to be the commodore's ship in the Training Squadron. For thirteen years she led the other corvettes, *Volage*, *Calypso* and *Rover*, on sail-training exercises, and was readily picked out from the others because her single topsails had four bands of reef points. She is reputed to have been the last square-rigged naval ship to leave Portsmouth Harbour under sail. Relieved by *Raleigh*, she paid off in 1898 and went into reserve, being sold out of the service in 1906.

HMS ACTIVE

HMS AGINCOURT

BATTLESHIP, LAUNCHED 1865, 400 FEET LONG, 10627 TONS

Armament	Four 9-inch MLR guns and twenty-four 7-inch MLR guns.
Armour	Sides 5½ inches.
Designer	Isaac Watts.
Builder	Laird Brothers, Birkenhead.
Horsepower	1350.
Speed	13½ knots, but 15.4 knots recorded.
Scrapped	Broken up at Grays, Essex in 1960.

This five-masted battleship, sister to *Minotaur,* was the largest single-screw fighting ship ever built. Its other claim to fame is that there were no transverse bulkheads on the main deck so that it was possible to stand in the eyes of the ship near the hawse-pipes and look down the whole length of the deck. As may be imagined, this open-plan way of living was not popular with the officers or the men.

In 1869, when first ready for sea, *Agincourt* had the unusual duty of teaming up with *Northumberland* to tow the Bermuda Floating Dock from the Thames to Madeira where *Warrior* and *Black Prince* would take over. *Agincourt* loaded full bunkers and stacked a further 500 tons of coal in bags on the gun deck. The two battleships towed in tandem – *Agincourt* leading – and made Madeira in eleven days.

She became the flagship of the second-in-command of the Channel Squadron, and in 1871 made the headlines on going aground on the Pearl Rock when leaving Gibraltar. Stuck fast for three days, she was eventually dragged off by the *Hercules* with the popular Lord Gilford in command. In 1877 *Agincourt* went as flagship of the second-in-command in the Mediterranean and was fitted with light quick-firing guns against torpedo attack. She took part in the show of strength at the Golden Horn in 1878, but then came home to serve again in the Channel Squadron. By 1889 the ship had been cut down to a three-masted barque and most of her guns were in store ashore. She lay at the head of the northern line at the Spithead Golden Jubilee Review of 1887, but paid off two years later.

Relegated to harbour service, *Agincourt* was first an accommodation ship at Portland and then was stripped to become coal hulk C.109 in the Medway. There was talk of saving her for posterity, but her armour had gone for scrap and there was very little left save the bare hull. She was towed to Grays for breaking up in 1960. Like so many Victorian battleships, she had not fired a single shot in anger.

HMS AGINCOURT

HMS ALEXANDRA

BATTLESHIP, LAUNCHED 1875, 325 FEET LONG, 9490 TONS

Armament	Two 11-inch MLR, ten 10-inch MLR and six 20-pounder BL guns originally, then the 11-inch guns and two of the 10- inch guns replaced by four 9.2-inch BL guns and the 20-pounders by six 4-inch BL guns.
Armour	12 inches amidships.
Designer	Nathaniel Barnaby.
Builder	Royal Dockyard, Chatham.
Horsepower	8312 Indicated Horsepower: twin screws.
Speed	14.8 knots, with 15 knots obtainable.
Scrapped	1908.

Last of the central battery ships, *Alexandra* was built of malleable iron, had a 6-foot ram and was reckoned a very dull sailer, never logging more than 6 knots under canvas. After 12 years in service the heavily-sparred barque rig was taken down and pole masts for signalling purposes substituted. Her muzzle-loading guns in the main battery were positioned above the boilers so that when the ready-use ammunition was exhausted further supplies had to be trolleyed or dragged from distant magazines and shell rooms. When this happened the gun-crews on the disengaged side had to help out as ammunition-passers.

The high point of her career came in 1882 when she fired the first shot during the bombardment of Alexandria, being hit in return about 60 times by enemy shore batteries. The Victoria Cross was awarded to Gunner Israel Harding for putting a live shell, its fuse still burning, into a tub of water. Her armour stood up remarkably well to the pounding, for although the range was a mere 1500 yards there were only four casualties.

Alexandra returned to England in 1889 to pay off, and after an extensive refit served for ten years as a flagship of the First Reserve Fleet. Based chiefly at Portland, her only forays into blue water took place during gunnery practice or the annual summer cruise. In 1901 she was reduced to being a mechanical training ship, and was broken up in 1908. She was the most massively-protected of all the battleships to assemble at Spithead in 1897 for Queen Victoria's Diamond Jubilee, and the only one still mainly armed with muzzle-loading guns.

HMS ALEXANDRA

HMS BACCHANTE

CORVETTE, LAUNCHED 1876, 280 FEET LONG, 4070 TONS

Armament	First, fourteen 7-inch MLR guns. Later, ten 7-inch MLR and four 6-inch BLR guns. Two 14-inch torpedo carriages.
Designer	Controller of the Navy.
Builder	Royal Dockyard, Portsmouth.
Horsepower	5420 Indicated Horsepower.
Speed	15 knots steam; 11½ knots under sail.
Scrapped	1897.

Sister to *Euryalus* and *Boadicea, Bacchante* was classified as a corvette although well able to do full duty as a cruiser. Her hull was of iron, clad with teak and zinc-sheathed; her compound engines were by Rennie and had a high-pressure cylinder placed between two low-pressure ones receiving steam from ten Scotch boilers at 70 pounds a square inch. With a speed of 15 knots, there was nothing then afloat that could escape from her. The displacement tonnage should have been 3932 tons, but in the event some extra ballast had to go in that brought her up to 4070 tons. She represented the last manifestation of the smaller broadside-armed vessel with everything in that broadside. She had, as a contemporary observed, all her teeth in the lower jaw.

Bacchante was ready for employment at the very moment when both sons of the future Edward VII were passing out from *Britannia* as very junior officers, and in 1880 *Bacchante* went off with the Royal Princes as part of the Detached Squadron showing the flag around the world. In two years she covered over 40 000 miles, mostly under sail, and rounded the Cape of Good Hope twice. She paid off at Portsmouth in 1882, and after a long refit and partial rearmament went out to relieve *Euryalus* as East Indies flagship. During the Burmese War of 1885 she transferred about three-quarters of her complement to serve on Irrawaddy river steamers 500 miles from sea or chasing dacoits through the jungle. Returning home in 1888, she lay in reserve until sold for scrap in 1897. She, and her sisters, were the last of the iron ships and the largest corvettes in the Royal Navy. She is also the only British vessel in which two grandsons of a sovereign served at the same time.

HMS BACCHANTE

HMS BELLEROPHON

BATTLESHIP, LAUNCHED 1865, 300 FEET LONG, 7551 TONS

Armament	Ten 9-inch and five 7-inch MLR guns originally, then ten 8-inch, four 6-inch and six 4-inch BLR guns.
Armour	Six inches at sides.
Designer	Edward James Reed.
Builder	Royal Dockyard, Chatham.
Horsepower	1000.
Speed	14.2 knots under her Penn engines and 10 knots under sail.
Scrapped	Broken up at Bo'ness in 1923.

She was, with *Hercules*, the first of the central battery ships. Short-hulled, and with all her heavy guns concentrated in a central battery protected by armour plate, the design was devised to take advantage of the new, larger forged iron, and steel, guns that were taking the place of cast iron weapons. This short battleship was built around a battery only ninety-eight feet long, and was much cheaper than, for example, the *Warrior* with greater displacement and finer lines. One disadvantage was that *Bellerophon* had such a low centre of gravity that she rolled heavily in a beam sea, while the bluff bows meant that she pushed so much water ahead of her that it was a standing joke that the flag-lieutenant used to report to the admiral that *Bellerophon's* bow wave was in sight long before the ship itself was visible.

The ship was five years in the Channel Squadron, and then served for a year in the Mediterranean. She came home to be fitted out as a foreign-station flagship, and in October 1873 set off for the West Indies. When under sail and a week out of Madeira there was a bizarre collision with a merchantman. She spotted the Liverpool steamer *Flamsteed* coming the other way and signalled for sight of their old newspapers. The master of the *Flamsteed* obligingly stopped while the battleship sent a boat. When the steamer was towing the boat back her master misjudged his distance and rammed the battleship, stoving in his bows. *Bellerophon* rushed working parties over, but it was to no avail, for the Liverpool ship sank after a few hours.

In 1892 *Bellerophon* came home from the North American station and in the following year became the port guardship at Pembroke Dock. In 1904 she was relegated to be a training hull for stokers at Plymouth under the name *Indus III* . Sold out of the service in 1922, she was broken up at Bo'ness in 1923.

HMS BELLEROPHON

HMS BOADICEA

CORVETTE, LAUNCHED 1875, 280 FEET LONG, 3913 TONS.

Armament	Originally, fourteen 7-inch MLR and two 64-pounder MLR guns. Later, two of the 7-inch guns changed to 6-inch BLR guns. Two 14-inch Whitehead torpedo carriages.
Designer	Controller of the Navy.
Builder	Royal Dockyard, Portsmouth.
Horsepower	5130 Indicated Horsepower.
Speed	14.8 knots.
Scrapped	Sold for breaking up in 1905.

The cruiser concept may be said to make a somewhat hesitant start with *Boadicea,* first of her class to see service. Iron-hulled and copper-sheathed for long-range work, her design was excellent in two respects – the machinery and the coal capacity. She was fitted with a horizontal return connecting-rod engine for two-stage expansion by J. & G. Rennie, and ten single-ended boilers supplied steam to a high-pressure cylinder 73 inches in diameter linked to two low-pressure cylinders and two condensers. On trials, the engine gave 14.8 knots at 74.5 revolutions a minute. A model of this first-rate engine may be seen at the Science Museum, Kensington, London. Her coal capacity was 540 tons – the same as the much larger *Raleigh* with whom *Boadicea* is often compared.

Shortly after completion she was sent under Commodore 'King Dick' Richards to the Cape of Good Hope and West African station for a tour of seven years. Her crew was often engaged ashore. In 1879 one of her seamen was manning a defence post at Inyezane when a small boy tumbled into it. The sailor cuffed him round the head and sat on him until the attack was over. The lad was adopted as ship's mascot, and later joined the Royal Navy. Two years later the commander, the gunnery lieutenant and nineteen men were killed at Laing's Neck and Majuba during the Transvaal affair. The most celebrated character associated with the ship in the 1890s was Vice-Admiral William Kennedy, whose passion was hunting. As flagship of the East India station, *Boadicea* should have steamed sedately between Aden, Bombay and Trincomalee, but 'Bill' Kennedy seems to have made sure that there were urgent reasons of state why the ship should be in Madagascar waters when the guinea-fowl were flying, or at Mauritius when a particularly big stag had been reported. In 1895 the ship came home to pay off, and in due course was sold for breaking up.

HMS BOADICEA

HMS CAPTAIN

BATTLESHIP, LAUNCHED 1869, 320 FEET LONG, 6950 TONS

Armament	Four 12-inch guns, two 7-inch guns.
Armour	Sides 8 inches, turrets 10 inches.
Designer	Cowper Coles.
Builder	Laird Brothers, Birkenhead.
Horsepower	900.
Speed	14.2 knots
Lost	Capsized during a Bay of Biscay gale in 1870.

Captain is the only British armoured vessel to have been lost through lack of sea-keeping qualities, and the explanation is that she was over-sparred, over-canvassed and had scarcely any freeboard. Cowper Coles, her designer, had been greatly influenced by the success of Ericsson's *Monitor* during the American Civil War and believed that the advantages of low freeboard – a reduced outline and less surface presented to the enemy guns – outweighed the disadvantages of being more at the mercy of the elements. He had wanted the ship to be mastless, but after the Admiralty objected he added three masts of the tripod variety and a full suit of sails. Fully loaded, she was 2 feet down on her marks and had barely 7 feet of freeboard in smooth water. In any kind of sea *Captain* was a mere half-tide rock, and her turrets were flooded with tons of water.

The design was manifestly a failure, but two of the ideas central to it were to blossom and grow. The main turrets revolved and were on the centre-line so that all the main armament could be directed to port or starboard, while twin screws for propulsion halved the risks attendant on engine breakdown. The construction of the *Captain* was an expression of a feeling that a ship should be designed around its weapons rather than have them fitted in afterwards: her loss was due to a lack of appreciation of other factors. A low freeboard meant that very little coal could be carried, and that meant a reliance on sail to get a decent radius of action. Cole's supreme confidence in his creation led to a demand for canvas on the first-class scale. The hull was just over 53 feet in the beam to the length of 320 feet, and the tripod masts, in place of more pliant shrouds of steel wire, carried a doubled amount of thrust. These are recipes for a capsize, and so quickly did she go down that only eighteen men were saved – Cowper Coles perishing with his ship.

HMS CAPTAIN

HMS CHALLENGER

CORVETTE, LAUNCHED 1858, 200 FEET LONG, 2290 TONS

Armament	Fitted with twenty-two guns as a warship, but these reduced to two for signalling purposes when the ship was selected for survey and discovery duties.
Builder	Royal Dockyard, Woolwich.
Horsepower	1200 Indicated Horsepower.
Speed	11 knots.
Scrapped	Broken up in 1921.

Challenger was a single-screw wooden ship, coppered below the waterline, and designed for the work of a small colonial cruiser. Commissioned in 1861, she served a tour of duty on the North American and West Indian station, and in 1866 was chosen as the commodore's ship by Captain Rochfort Maguire on the Australian station. She was an excellent sailer, which may have been the reason for her suitability in Australian waters where coal depots were few and far between.

In 1872 she sailed from Sheerness on an epic voyage of oceanographic and scientific research that would carry her over 68 000 miles. Her captain was George Nares, later to achieve fame as the leader of the Arctic expedition of *Discovery* and *Alert*, and the scientific party of naturalists, a chemist, a physicist and a photographer was headed by Professor Wyville Thomson. The primary purpose of the voyage was an exploration of the depths of the sea, and to that end the work of dredging and trawling went on day and night for more than 3 years. The notes on the expedition filled 50 volumes and took 10 years to publish.

Many accounts of the voyage were written, and the best of them turned out to be H.N. Moseley's *Notes by a Naturalist* which was not about the primary purpose of the voyage at all but dealt with the lands and islands visited by *Challenger*. It may fairly be compared to Darwin's *Voyage of H.M.S. Beagle*, for both naturalists shared the gift of accurate observation, and Moseley's book became a minor late-Victorian classic.

The later fate of *Challenger* was ignominious, for the Hydrographer of the Navy, who had authorised her employment, now found her too large and too expensive to use on orthodox surveys. She became a mooring hulk at Chatham in 1880, but was not broken up until 1921.

HMS CHALLENGER

HMS COMUS

CORVETTE, LAUNCHED 1878, 225 FEET LONG, 2380 TONS

Armament	Two 7-inch and twelve 64-pounder MLR guns at first, then four 6-inch BLR and eight 64-pounder MLR guns, eight machine guns and two torpedo carriages.
Designer	Nathaniel Barnaby.
Builder	J. Elder & Co., Glasgow.
Horsepower	2450 Indicated Horsepower.
Speed	13 knots.
Scrapped	Sold for breaking up in 1904.

The first 'C'-class corvettes of the *Comus* type were launched between April and October 1878, and the six were called *Carysfort, Champion, Cleopatra, Conquest, Curacoa* and *Comus* . They were built to replace worn-out tonnage and to counter the French ships *Primauguet, D' Estaing* and *La Perouse* which had the same displacement. France's main interests were in the Mediterranean, and these last-named ships could afford to put sail in second place; *Comus* and her sisters had to face long oceanic voyages with bunkering stops few and far between, and a beamy hull for sail-carrying was essential. As a result, one can say that *Comus* is up on broadside with 700 pounds of shell to the French 492 while *La Perouse*, for example, is two knots faster. In boxing terms, *Comus* had the punch, *La Perouse* the legs.

Comus was commissioned in 1879 for the China station, and from there she moved to the Pacific, coming home in 1884 for a refit and change of armament. Between 1886 and 1891 she was on the North American and West Indies station, and from 1895 to 1898 was back in the Pacific. In 1896 her marines and seamen had the unusual experience of landing in Nicaragua to sort out a wrangle between politicians and a British bank as to whether a loan was forced or voluntary. After a final tour in the Americas, *Comus* came home in 1900 and went into reserve at Devonport. Struck off the active list in 1902, she was sold for breaking up in 1904. The class had been a stop-gap provision with each ship as expensive, ton for ton, as the largest ironclad. A contemporary observer put the matter in a nutshell. ' The *Comus* class' he said, 'through deficiency of speed are practically unavailable for the protection of commerce.'

HMS COMUS

HM Indian Troop Ship
CROCODILE

TROOPSHIP, LAUNCHED 1867, 360 FEET LONG, 6211 TONS

Armament	Three 4-pounder guns.
Designer	Controller of the Navy.
Builder	Wigram, Blackwall.
Horsepower	700.
Speed	9 knots.
Scrapped	Disposed of in 1896 for breaking up.

The Admiralty had been alarmed at the difficulties experienced in securing enough shipping of the right type to move soldiers and sailors around the world during the Crimean War and the Indian Mutiny, and Rowley Richardson made the suggestion that the Royal Navy should build and operate five troopships on behalf of the Indian Government. The criteria were to be that each ship should be able to carry a full battalion of infantry, with married families and auxiliaries, or 1200 men. The five ships were *Crocodile, Euphrates, Serapis, Jumna* and *Malabar,* and each bore the Star of India in gold on the bow. They were painted with distinctive bands on the hull to aid identification at a distance. *Crocodile* had a yellow or buff band to distinguish her from *Euphrates* (blue), *Serapis* (green), *Jumna* (red), and *Malabar* (black). Before the opening of the Suez Canal, *Crocodile* and *Serapis* ran from England to Alexandria, and the other three from Suez to Bombay.

The accommodation acquired a set of nicknames over the years. Married ladies with babies lived on the deck below the saloon, and their part of the ship was called ' The Nursery'. Unmarried ladies on the same deck, but in an easily-segregated corner, inhabited ' The Dovecot'. Unmarried subalterns languished uncomfortably below the water line in ' The Pandemonium'. The NCOs and men were tucked into even less salubrious quarters, but they had the benefit of a dram of navy rum daily, while the *Crocodile* was reputed to have the best food. The ship, however, was both slow and increasingly overcrowded as the numbers crept up to 1800 a voyage. In 1894 four of the five naval troopers were laid up while two P&O ships, *Victoria* and, *Britannia,* had a trial as troopers on charter. The two newcomers soon demonstrated that they could make a better job of it than the old naval ships, and *Crocodile* and her sisters were disposed of in 1896.

HMS CROCODILE

33

HMS CRUISER

SLOOP, LAUNCHED 1852, 160 FEET LONG, 1073 TONS

Armament	Seventeen 32-pounder guns – later removed.
Builder	Royal Dockyard, Deptford.
Scrapped	Sold out of the service at Malta in 1912.

The picture by Mitchell of this ship is one that he may have composed from a photograph, sketch or description, for *Cruiser* was never in Portsmouth after 1872, and the background indicates that she is off Malta. This little ship had an interesting and long life that falls into two distinct parts.

A wooden screw sloop with an auxiliary horizontal-geared engine by J. & G. Rennie, she began life as *Cruizer* and had the name changed to *Cruiser* in 1857. Her first few years were spent in Chinese waters, and a party of her men in boats took part in the Battle of Fatshan Creek in 1857. Her captain, Commander Charles Fellowes, was the first man over the walls of Canton when the city was taken, and the ship was further engaged in fighting up the Yang-tse in 1858 while her men took part in the attack on the Peiho Forts in 1859. In 1860, under Commander John Bythesea, her crew surveyed the Gulf of Pechili so as to prepare the mooring of the allied fleet that was to disembark troops for the advance to Peking.

On returning to England *Cruiser* was laid up until 1867 when she was re-commissioned for the Mediterranean station. In 1872, having shed her guns and engine, she became a sail-training ship with the primary function of giving young officers and seamen experiences in handling square-rigged sailing craft. She had all the extras that such work entails; stunsails, single topsails with four bands of reefing points and a Jimmy Green set between the end of the bowsprit and the dolphin striker to help her head pay off in light weather. Admiral Ballard recalls in his memoirs that in the 1880s she was commanded by Commander 'Bully' Darwin, a corpulent but first-rate seaman of the old school who had a voice like a bull and who would not suffer fools gladly. The ship continued in commission into the twentieth-century under the name *Lark* and seems to have been still in service in 1903, being sold at Malta for breaking up in 1912.

HMS CRUISER

HMS DEFENCE

BATTLESHIP, LAUNCHED 1861, 280 FEET LONG, 6070 TONS

Armament	Two 8-inch and fourteen 7-inch MLR guns (after first commission).
Armour	Sides 4½ inches.
Designer	Baldwin Walker.
Builder	Palmer's, Jarrow.
Horsepower	600.
Speed	11.23 knots, but once recorded 11.62 knots. Under sail, 10½ knots.
Scrapped	Sold out of the service in 1935.

The *Defence*, and the *Resistance*, were popularly known as 'steam rams' because they had been built with prominent bow projections shaped a little like ploughshares. Laid down only a few months after *Warrior*, they illustrated the fuzzy thinking reigning at the Admiralty. The ram had been a success at Lissa, but the truth was that these fearsome underwater beaks menaced chiefly one's own ships. Ram bows became fashionable, however, and did not begin to go out of favour until the mid-1890s. When the *Camperdown* sank the *Victoria* in 1893 and drowned the Commander-in-Chief the seamen nicknamed the surviving ship 'Crampherdown' and muttered uneasily whenever it took up station astern. The naval architects put no more rams on armoured fighting ships after World War One.

The classification of *Defence* as a battleship may seem a little strange nowadays, for although she was a three-decker the engines put into the hull were those of the frigate, while on her maiden commission she bore the chequered sides of the Victorian frigate. Her initial layout was on frigate lines consisting of ten 68-pounder SB guns on the main deck with split topsail rig on an experimental basis. With her new all-rifled armament, single topsail, fiddled topgallant masts and a run-in bowsprit she did at least look more like a battleship.

Defence was eight years with the Channel Squadron and then spent a year in the Mediterranean before transferring as flagship to the North American station. She was two years a guardship in Ireland, did a second spell with the Channel Squadron and was present when Cyprus came under the British flag. After another spell as a guardship in the Mersey she was laid up at Plymouth in 1885. A final period of service began in 1890 when, re-named *Indus* , she was moored in the Hamoaze as a training ship. There she lay for 45 years until sold for scrapping in 1935.

HMS DEFENCE

HMS DEVASTATION

BATTLESHIP, LAUNCHED 1871, 285 FEET LONG, 9330 TONS

Armament	Four 12-inch MLR guns initially, then in 1891 fitted four 10-inch BLR guns.
Armour	Turrets had 12-14 inches, hull 8-12 inches.
Designer	Edward James Reed.
Builder	Royal Dockyard, Portsmouth.
Horsepower	800.
Speed	13.3 knots.
Scrapped	Sold for breaking up in 1908.

Devastation, and *Dreadnought*, were built as turret ships without the heavy tripod masts, excessive top hamper and low freeboard that had led to the loss of *Captain*, and *Devastation* may fairly lay claim to have been the first mastless capital ship. Her turrets could train through an arc of 280° and she was such good propaganda for the pro-Navy element in society that the intrepid Phipps Hornby, now an admiral, took her on a round-Britain cruise. An Aberdeen dancing-master composed the 'Devastation Galop' in honour of a visit by the ship, but it is recorded that the crew were not pleased with their accommodation. When a journalist asked what it was like below a grizzled seaman responded that is was like living in 'ratholes with tinned air!'

A ship without sails was a novelty in the 1870s, and so was one with all her her main armament on top of the hull instead of inside it. She had a flat bottom, a pointed ram and square bilges. Her uncompromising appearance was such that it was popularly believed that she was the model for the warship appearing on boxes of 'England's Glory' matches but, as with the instance of the sailor depicted on packets of Players' cigarettes, the truth behind such folk-lore is hard to discern.

Relying as she did on four big guns, it was necessary when the torpedo scare took place to arm her with a battery of quick-firers and two torpedo carriages. When, in 1891, her main armament was changed to four 10-inch guns her firepower was actually raised. The lower-calibre guns had three times the rate of fire and threw a 500-pound shell twice the range. For all that, her service career was uneventful. *Devastation* was in the Mediterranean, then on reserve. She became a guardship at Plymouth, Gibraltar and in Scotland, finally paying off in 1902 and being broken up in 1908. It does not rob her of her place in history as the first mastless capital ship –the first to take no account of the wind for propulsion.

HMS DEVASTATION

HMS DIAMOND

CORVETTE, LAUNCHED 1874, 220 FEET LONG, 1970 TONS

Armament	Fourteen 64-pounder MLR guns of two types (see text) and later reduced to twelve.
Designer	Controller of the Navy.
Builder	Royal Dockyard, Sheerness.
Horsepower	2155 Indicated Horsepower.
Speed	13 knots.
Scrapped	Sold out of the service in 1889.

Wooden shipbuilding in royal dockyards came to an end with the construction of what is commonly, but wrongly, called the 'Gem-class corvettes'. Their names were *Amethyst, Diamond, Encounter, Modeste* and *Sapphire*, and *Diamond* was the fourth to be built and launched. Coppered below the waterline, she did the work of a third-class colonial cruiser and was originally armed with fourteen guns, six a side and one each at bow and stern.

Her armament was an interesting feature for this late date, for these wooden ships were not given breech-loaders but fitted with two types of muzzle-loaders. On her first commission, *Diamond* bore rifled guns adapted from surplus smooth-bore barrels. A cavalry officer called Palliser invented a rifled steel tube that would take a 64-pound projectile and fit into an old 58-cwt gun. The practical effect was a doubling of the penetration and range of the projectile at a third of the cost of new weapons. These converted guns were on wooden truck carriages, but after the 1880 refit they were replaced by ten of the newer and lighter 64-pounders mounted on iron slides and having a faster rate of fire.

Diamond went out to the East Indies in 1875, and from there to the China station, coming home in 1879. After a refit she was seven and a half years in Australian waters, paying off in 1889 and being sold out of the service in the same year. With a full ship rig, *Diamond* could sail as fast as she could steam, and it is on record that she was the last large square-rigged ship to undertake the intricate navigation of the Rangoon estuary under sail alone.

HMS DIAMOND

HMS DISCOVERY

STORESHIP, LAUNCHED 1873, 160 FEET LONG, 1250 TONS

Designer	Alexander Stephens and Sons, Dundee.
Builder	Alexander Stephens and Sons, Dundee.
Horsepower	365 Indicated Horsepower.
Scrapped	Sold for break up in 1902.

Originally named *Bloodhound* and built as an Arctic steam whaler, the ship was purchased by the Royal Navy in 1874 and re-named *Discovery*. The background was that Disraeli had been forced to give in to pressure from a lobby in the House of Commons that was pushing for a renewal of an assault on the Arctic. The thrust of the argument was threefold. National honour required that the failure of the Franklin expedition be wiped from the record; a north-west passage might yet be found with possible commercial advantages and the North Pole could be reached. A leading protagonist, Sherard Osborn, also thought it might do something for Navy morale, for he spoke scornfully of a Navy that was 'for ever crossing topgallant yards and cleaning brasswork'. The Admiralty was eventually persuaded; the Royal Geographical Society concurred and what became known as the Nares Expedition was launched. The official object was to attain the highest possible northern latitude, and perhaps have a shot at reaching the North Pole.

Two ships were employed; the *Discovery* commanded by Captain Henry Stephenson, and the *Alert* under George Nares who had left the *Challenger* expedition for the purpose. Two years' provisions were stowed away; husky dog teams and two Greenlanders were recruited. Sailing from Portsmouth, *Discovery* wintered in Lady Franklin Sound while the *Alert* went a little further north and a land party penetrated hummocky ice to get to 83° 20' N – 400 miles from the North Pole. Eventually, Nares sent a short telegram, 'Pole impracticable; no land to northward', and the ships set off for home, reaching England in October 1876. *Discovery* had been embedded in ice for ten and a half months but had come to little harm.

Alert subsequently went surveying in Patagonia, but *Discovery* had little further use and was hulked, being finally sold for breaking up in 1902. She was, of course, not Scott's Antarctic ship *Discovery* which was moored for many years on the Thames Embankment and is still afloat as a museum ship in Dundee.

HMS DISCOVERY

HMS DREADNOUGHT

BATTLESHIP, LAUNCHED 1875, 320 FEET LONG, 10 886 TONS.

Armament	Four 12½-inch MLR guns.
Armour	Complete. It was from 10-14 inches amidships, 14 inches on the turrets, skin 1½ inches and 2½–3 inches on the decks.
Designers	As *Fury*, Edward James Reed. As *Dreadnought*, William Henry White and Nathaniel Barnaby.
Builders	Pembroke Royal Dockyard.
Horsepower	8206 Indicated Horsepower.
Speed	14 knots.
Scrapped	Sold for breaking up in 1908.

Originally intended to bear the name *Fury* , this twin-screw ship had the thickest complete belt of armour of any British warship, and her building was a muddled affair extending over almost seven years. Reed has designed her with a low bow, 12-inch guns and a citadel standing well inboard. White and Barnaby built her up fore and aft, took the citadel out to the sides of the hull and put in heavier guns and armour plate.

For some years she had no other armament except the 12½-inch guns, but in 1885 ten Nordenfelts were mounted on the hurricane deck, to be replaced in 1894 by 3-pounders and 6-pounders. Her compound engines required high-pressure cylinders, and these were installed vertically so that the former convention that cylinders be put in horizontally and below the waterline for protection was now dropped. Two other innovations were a longitudinal bulkhead dividing the engine room from the boiler room, and artificial ventilation. This latter development followed reports from the *Devastation*, the same ship from which came the seaman's grumble that living below was like being in 'ratholes with tinned air'.

Commissioned in 1879 for trails, *Dreadnought* was in reserve at Portsmouth until 1884 when she went out to the Mediterannean for ten uneventful years. There followed a spell as a coastguard ship in Ireland, and in 1902 she joined *Defiance* at Devonport as a tender and torpedo boat depot ship, going into dockyard reserve in 1905. She was sold in July 1908 for £23 000 – about 4% of her construction cost.

HMS DREADNOUGHT

HMS DUKE OF WELLINGTON

BATTLESHIP, LAUNCHED 1852, 250 FEET LONG, 3471 TONS

Armament	131 SB guns of mixed calibre, reduced to 23 for signalling and ceremonial purposes.
Builder	Pembroke Royal Dockyard.
Horsepower	700.
Speed	10.7 knots.
Scrapped	Sold in 1904 and broken up at Charlton.

Launched as the *Windsor Castle* on the day that the Duke of Wellington died, she was given the name of the victor of Waterloo, and a new figurehead, in his memory. One of the last of the wooden walls, it has been calculated that an oak forest of 76 acres of trees had been cleared to build her. Nine-tenths of the way through the construction process it was decided to put an engine in her, and the hull was sawn apart so that an extra 20 feet could be inserted to take the machinery and boilers for a Robert Napier steam engine driving a single screw.

Vice-Admiral Sir Charles Napier chose *Duke of Wellington* to be his flagship in the Baltic at the outbreak of the Crimean War, and he based himself at Kiel at first because the Admiralty had forbidden him to attack the fortresses of Sveaborg or Kronstadt or do anything more than block the exit to the Baltic. In the first months of war this was probably a wise direction, for Napier's men were mostly landsmen and pensioners signed-on in haste, while his fleet was deep-draught and armed with ship-to-ship weapons when what was wanted was shallow-draught vessels armed with mortars. When the ice cleared he sent ships forward, and they reported that Kronstadt was impregnable, and Sveaborg impossible. He turned his attention to Bomarsund in the Aland Islands, and bare-footed seamen dragged 32-pounders on sledges for miles to batter the granite fortress. It surrendered after four days, and Napier returned to England in *Duke of Wellington* in December 1854. He had only lost three men in taking Bomarsund, but the Admiralty had not liked his interpretation of instructions, or his brusque reports, and he was ordered to strike his flag.

Duke of Wellington remained at Portsmouth as guardship, receiving ship and flagship for almost half a century. In 1869 she replaced *Victory* as flagship, and the roles were not reversed again until 1891. In her last years *Duke of Wellington* was a depot ship, roofed over to keep out the rain and rot, and tethered permanently to the quayside until towed away to be broken up in 1904.

HMS DUKE OF WELLINGTON

HMS ENTERPRISE

SLOOP, LAUNCHED 1864, 180 FEET LONG, 1530 TONS

Armament	Two 100-pounder SB and two 110-pounder ML guns on first Mediterranean commission; then four 7-inch MLR guns.
Armour	A belt of iron plate 4½ inches thick from three feet below the load line to the upper deck.
Designer	Edward James Reed.
Builder	Royal Dockyard, Deptford.
Horsepower	160.
Speed	9.9 knots.
Scrapped	Sold out of the service in 1885–86.

This ship may be said to be the first 'pocket battleship', for it mounted four very large guns in a tiny hull. Laid down as the 17-gun sloop *Circassian*, Reed said he would make her 'our first small ironclad' by putting iron plating on a wooden hull and installing four heavy guns in a box battery amidships. *Enterprise* had a short life, serving only 7 years in active commission. She had a change of armament at Malta in 1868 when four 7-inch MLR guns were put in as replacements. Their arc of fire, however, was severely restricted, and when she paid off in 1871 *Enterprise* went into reserve until being sold for scrap in 1885–86. She serves as a symbol of the Admiralty's indecision over the merits of iron and wood in the early 1860s.

HMS COMET

COAST DEFENCE GUNBOAT, LAUNCHED 1870, 85 FEET LONG, 245 TONS

Armament	One 10-inch MLR gun.
Designer	Controller of the Navy.
Builder	Royal Dockyard, Portsmouth.
Horsepower	60.
Speed	8.7 knots.
Scrapped	Sold in 1908 and broken up in Holland.

These Rennie-engined, twin screw vessels were a class of twenty with some faintly comical names like *Ant*, *Cuckoo*, *Hyaena* and *Snake*. As third-class gunboats, they represented the smallest group of armed vessels and had a crew of only 25 men. The lineal descendants in iron of the wooden gunboats used in the Crimean War, their role was defensive rather than offensive and they were more often in reserve than in service. *Comet* grew slower with age, and in 1898 could only make four knots. She was sold in 1908 and broken up in Holland.

HMS ENTERPRISE & HMGB COMET

HM Ships
EXCELLENT, CALCUTTA AND VERNON

These roofed-over hulks were moored together in Fountain Lake between Portsmouth Dockyard and the emerging Whale Island, which was being built up by gangs of grey-clad convicts with mud taken from dockyard excavations. *Excellent*, which was joined by a walkway to *Calcutta* (left and centre in Mitchell's drawing), was the school of gunnery, while *Vernon* (and another hulk *Ariadne*, not in the picture) were the torpedo school. The names *Excellent* and *Vernon* are continuing titles for the schools, and the *Excellent* shown here is the *Queen Charlotte* of 104 guns which had been launched in 1810.

Young officers and seamen were instructed in theory and practice aboard the two gunnery hulks, and *Excellent* carried ten 9-inch SB guns which fired solid shot across the mudflats at half tide when the water was too low for boats and too high for shrimpers or bait diggers. The local longshoremen made their beer money by salvaging such shot as they could find and selling them back to the Navy at a farthing a pound. On her upper deck she carried a 40-pounder Armstrong BLR gun, but this was never fired. For turret work pupils used the coastal defence ship *Glatton* which lay on a near-by buoy.

Vernon had been a smart 50-gun frigate, but now carried no guns and was a warren of lecture rooms and accommodation space below decks. Students were taught to handle spar torpedoes – a form of contact mine on a pole stuck out over the bow of small craft – and Whitehead torpedoes with a speed of 19 knots. The latter had a range of only a few hundred yards and were recovered by rowing boat.

With the passage of time *Excellent* as an institution moved ashore to Whale Island and the hulks were broken up. *Vernon* also moved ashore, but the hulk tradition lasted a little longer in her case. In the 1940s there were still two old battleships lashed together in Portsmouth Harbour functioning as an accommodation and instructional unit under the name of *Vernon II*.

HM SHIPS EXCELLENT, CALCUTTA & VERNON

HMS FALCON

GUN VESSEL, LAUNCHED 1877, 157 FEET LONG, 780 TONS

Armament	One 7-inch and two 6-inch MLR guns.
Designer	Controller of the Navy.
Builder	Lairds, Birkenhead.
Horsepower	721 Indicated Horsepower.
Speed	11 knots.
Scrapped	Sold out of the service in 1920.

Falcon, and *Griffon* were identical sisters in a class of gun-vessels usually known as the *Condor* type from the most famous of them all. *Falcon* differed from *Condor* in having a knee bow added after her second commission. *Falcon* retained her armament unchanged throughout her life, although it would be proper to say that her 6-inch guns were known as 64-pounders when installed. The 7-inch gun was positioned between the funnel and the mainmast, and one 64-pounder was in the bows; the other in the stern.

With a crew of about a hundred, *Falcon* was barque-rigged and could make about the same speed under her 13 000 square feet of canvas as under steam. She had ten years of active service, all of it in the Mediterranean fleet. She arrived on station in time to take part in the show of strength off Constantinople during the war between Russia and Turkey, and made several forays into the Black Sea. These were dangerous days under the loosening rule of the Sultans, and in the early part of her second commission the captain of *Falcon*, Commander Selby, was murdered by brigands while ashore shooting snipe. The ship went on patrol in the Suez Canal in 1882, and in 1885 was present at the siege of Suakin by the Mahdi's men.

In 1888 the ship came home to pay off at Plymouth, and thereafter lay dismantled in reserve until 1891 when she was selected to be a hulk on the torpedo range. *Falcon* was sold out the service for breaking up in 1920. Although she was originally intended for the China station, a chance diversion due to a political threat meant that she spent all her working life west of Aden.

HMS FALCON

HMS GLATTON

HARBOUR DEFENCE SHIP, LAUNCHED 1871, 245 FEET LONG, 4900 TONS

Armament	Two twelve-inch MLR guns (see text for later addition).
Armour	10–12 inches on topsides; 12–14 inches on turret.
Designer	Edward James Reed.
Building	Royal Dockyard, Chatham.
Horsepower	2870 Indicated Horsepower.
Speed	12.1 knots.
Scrapped	Sold out of the service in 1903.

The Admiralty requirement was for a 'low monitor of moderate speed', and Reed followed their instructions without much enthusiasm, commenting later that 'there is no vessel with the objects of which I am less acquainted than the *Glatton*'. In July 1872, before she had been commissioned, *Glatton* was the subject of an interesting test of her turret armour, and the quality of naval gunnery. *Hotspur* fired three 12-inch shells at the turret from 200 yards. The first one missed altogether; the second displaced a plate at the line of junction and remained embedded there, while the third struck the glacis, penetrated the turret plating to a depth of 15 inches and broke up. *Glatton's* turret had no interior damage, and worked perfectly immediately afterwards.

She was thus the best-protected breastwork monitor of her time, but suffered from low freeboard and having no means of firing astern. In all essentials, she was Ericsson's ship made four times larger, and just as vulnerable to the weather. On a good day she could go out as *Excellent's* gunnery tender and conduct a shoot, but her range was severely limited. In her whole career *Glatton* went as far afield as Portland in one direction and the Thames in the other. Most of the time was spent swinging round the buoy in Portsmouth Harbour, and she was so deficient in living-space that there was scarcely room to sleep her 200-odd officers and men on board.

Nevertheless, the Navy made the best use of her as a defence ship that circumstances allowed, for in 1881 torpedo carriages were fitted, and we know from old photographs that some light guns were added in 1896 – presumably to cover the vulnerable stern sector. Like an old actress forced to accept smaller and smaller parts, she moved slowly down the list, Second Class Reserve in 1889, Fleet Reserve in 1896 and Dockyard Reserve in 1901, being sold for scrap in 1903.

HMS GLATTON

HMS HECLA

TORPEDO BOAT DEPOT SHIP, LAUNCHED 1878, 392 FEET
LONG, 6400 TONS

Armament	Five 64-pounder MLR guns, one 5-inch and one 40-pounder BLR guns and four fixed torpedo tubes.
Builder	Harland and Wolff, Belfast.
Horsepower	1760 Indicated Horsepower.
Speed	12 knots.
Scrapped	Sold for breaking up in 1926.

Purchased as the merchant ship hull *British Crown* in 1878, *Hecla's* role in the Royal Navy was to be a carrier of mines and torpedoes and to be mothership to six second-class torpedo boats. Her normal sphere of operation in peacetime was to be based at Berehaven in summer and Malta in winter, and run courses all the year round for torpedomen. *Hecla* also went at regular intervals to Fiume to collect new stocks from the Whitehead factory. At the bombardment of Alexandria she delivered extra ammunition to the gun vessels shelling the Mex lines. Her captain, Arthur Wilson, went ashore with a 40-pounder after the troops landed and used it as part of the armoured train. Two years later the men of *Hecla* participated in the defence of Suakin and the advance to Khartoum. Wilson was awarded a Victoria Cross for his bravery at the action at Tamai, and in due course rose to be an Admiral of the Fleet.

Hecla was joined in her work by *Vulcan* in 1899, and the old ship was modernized and re-built in 1912 with a new displacement tonnage of 5600 and a more powerful engine. She had an extremely long life, and Admiral George Ballard records that she was the only ship that he had known as a Midshipman and an Admiral.

The second-class torpedo boat appearing in the foreground of Mitchell's illustration was built by John Thornycroft and Co. Ltd. at their Chiswick works. This particular specimen appears to be a prototype without an operable carriage for discharging torpedoes or tubes. The torpedoes of 1880 were 14 ½ feet long, carried 32 pounds of explosive, had a range of about 600 yards and speed of about nineteen knots. Fears as to the domination of the seas by these craft were set at rest in 1893 when the first torpedo-boat destroyer *Havock* was laid down. The torpedo did not gain advantage again until gyroscopic control was invented some 3 years later.

TORPEDO BOAT, 2ND CLASS & HMS HECLA

HMS HERCULES

BATTLESHIP, LAUNCHED 1868, 325 FEET LONG, 8677 TONS

Armament	Eight 10-inch, two 9-inch and four 7-inch MLR guns.
Armour	9 inches on sides, reducing to 5 inches.
Designer	Edward James Reed.
Builder	Royal Dockyard, Chatham.
Horsepower	1200.
Speed	13.8 knots.
Scrapped	Broken up at Preston in 1932.

Constructed on the same general lines as *Bellerophon.* she embodied many improvements. Her cables led in to the upper deck, she was faster and commanded the area immediately ahead with a bow gun run out through the stempost at main deck level. Her 9-inch armour was the thickest in existence at the time of her completion, and her Penn engines were powerful enough to pull *Agincourt* from the Pearl Rock in 1871 when every other expedient had failed. It was felt by contemporaries that she was at a disadvantage in having guns of three calibres – 10-inch, 9-inch and 7-inch – but only one change took place in the following years. In 1892 a pair of the 7-inch guns under the topgallant fo'c'sle were replaced by 6-inch breech-loaders. She was re-engined by the Greenock Foundry Company and eight cylindrical steel boilers were installed so that steam pressure could be raised significantly.

A long career in the Channel Squadron and as a Mediterranean flagship and Reserve Fleet flagship had preceded the 1892 modernisation, but thereafter she spent most of the time swinging round the buoy in Portsmouth. Her guns had not been comprehensively renewed, and in 1905 – despite the money spent on re-engining – *Hercules* was sent off to Gibraltar as an accommodation ship, being named *Calcutta* in 1909. Towed home in 1914, there followed a period as an artificers' training ship under the name *Fisgard II.* In 1932 she was sold for demolition. *Hercules* had been afloat over 60 years, and the design was closely followed for *Sultan* which was built immediately after *Hercules* had vacated the dock at Chatham. Of all the ships designed by Reed, *Hercules* may be said to have been his masterpiece, while in her latter years she serves to illustrate the 'partial modernisation' policy of the 1890s. The judgement of history must be that putting in new engines but keeping old guns does not give a second line of battle, as was hoped, but merely clutters up dockyard basins with sub-standard ships and wasted men.

HMS HERCULES

HMS HIMALAYA

TROOPSHIP, LAUNCHED 1853, 340 FEET LONG, 4690 TONS

Designer	T. Waterman.
Builder	Mare, Blackwall.
Horsepower	2500 Indicated Horsepower at 56 r.p.m.
Speed	13.7 knots.
Lost	Sunk by German aircraft at Portland in 1940.

Intended for construction as an iron paddler, the directors of the Peninsular & Oriental Steam Navigation Company who ordered the ship had a last minute change of mind and decided on a single-screw iron ship. On completion, she was the largest passenger ship afloat, and on her maiden voyage she was six and a half days from Southampton to Gibraltar, just over three days to Malta, and two and a half days thence to Alexandria. These were record passages for every lap of the voyage.

The owners now had cold feet, for they had committed a great deal of money to building and fitting-out *Himalaya* and could not see how she could pay dividends because of the heavy coal consumption and meagre freight potential. There was trouble brewing in the Black Sea, leading eventually to war, and the ship was chartered by the government to carry troops, first from Gibraltar to Constantinople and then from Queenstown to the Crimea. Her capacity was 1850 soldiers, and in 1855 the government bought the ship for about what P&O had paid for it, stipulating only that her engineers stay with her for a year. Later, the ship was taken over by the Royal Navy, painted white, and operated for almost 30 years carrying troops to garrisons abroad and seamen to relieve ships on foreign stations. As the years went by various extra accommodation was built into her so that her original steam-yacht silhouette became more matronly and less clearly defined.

Paid off in the mid-1890s, *Himalaya* was first coal hulk C.60 at Devonport, and then a refuelling ship in the Medway. She ended her days at Portland as a coal hulk, being sunk by German Junkers 88 aircraft in 1940. Her masts remained above water in the centre of the harbour until clearance of the wreck by a salvage company after World War Two.

HMS HIMALAYA

HMS HOTSPUR

COAST DEFENCE SHIP, LAUNCHED 1870, 235 FEET LONG, 4000 TONS

Armament	One 12-inch MLR gun and two 6 inch MLR guns at first, then two 12-inch MLR guns as main armament and two 6-inch BLR guns.
Armour	7–11 inches on sides, 10 inches on turret.
Designer	Edward James Reed.
Builder	Napier & Sons, Glasgow.
Horsepower	600.
Speed	12.8 knots.
Scrapped	Sold out of the service in 1904.

Designed as a fleet ram and then deployed for harbour defence, *Hotspur* had nevertheless the freeboard of an ocean-going ship, and that gave her advantages over ships like, for example, *Glatton* which could neither house all her crew nor steam safely to a foreign station. *Hotspur* spent some years in the Mediterranean and as a coastguard ship in various parts of Britain. Her engines drove twin screws, but she could only carry 300 tons of coal and was limited to seventy hours at maximum speed in calm water. It was enough, however, to keep an inexpensive, but seemingly well-armed and armoured, vessel in full commission for much of her service, even though low power and a tubby hull kept her virtually stationary in a head sea

The original armament was a 12-inch gun in a *fixed* turret with the weapon brought to one of four ports for firing. The turntable was hand-operated, and the gun had to be run-in to change the field of fire. In 1883 this arrangement was replaced by a revolving turret containing two 12-inch guns, with two of the new 6-inch breech-loaders covering the stern. Some quick-firers were added, and in 1887 *Hotspur* was fitted with torpedo nets. The idea was that a heavy metalled skirt, strung out on massive wooden outriggers, would defeat a torpedo attack but as the ship could hardly make any way with this armoured curtain dragging in the water the experiment was discontinued. Torpedo nets had a place when fleets were massed at anchorages, but major ships had then to rely on patrolling picket boats to give warning of possible attack by fast craft or, in later years, submarines.

Sold out of the service in 1904, *Hotspur* had been a popular draft because of her ample living space and relative immobility when on a foreign station. She had been described as an Iron Armour-Plated Ram when first launched, but it seems unlikely that a ship that had to screw down her safety valves to get eleven knots in her middle years could have moved quickly enough to ram a potential enemy.

HMS HOTSPUR

HMS INCONSTANT

FRIGATE, LAUNCHED 1868, 337 FEET LONG, 5780 TONS

Armament	Ten 9-inch and six 7-inch MLR guns.
Designer	Robert Spencer Robinson and Edward James Reed.
Builder	Pembroke Royal Dockyard.
Horsepower	1000 Nominal: 7360 Indicated Horsepower.
Speed	16.2 knots steam: 13.5 knots sail.
Scrapped	Broken up in 1956.

Inconstant was a fast steam frigate designed to hunt down commerce raiders of the *Alabama* or *Wampanoag* type, and the collective brainchild of the abrasive Controller of the Navy, Robert Spencer Robinson, and the evil-tempered Edward James Reed, Chief Constructor. This forceful, brilliant but unpopular pair had the vision of a fast, unarmoured ship with a few heavy, long-range guns, and able to operate for long periods without docking. Versions of the type in this book are *Shah*, *Raleigh*, *Volage* and *Active*.

Commissioned in 1869, *Inconstant* had the rare combination of high speed under steam and sail, being capable of over 16 knots under her Penn trunk engines and 13½ knots under sail. She began service with the Channel Squadron, and was next astern of *Captain* when the latter went down. In 1871 she was flagship of the Detached or Flying Squadron sent off to show the flag around the world. On the way back, at Cape Town, there took place a court martial that illustrates graphically the severity of naval discipline at the time. A marine serving in the ship had struck out at a sergeant who taunted him about his wife's fidelity; the would-be assailant got 14 year's hard labour on the breakwater as his punishment.

Paid off 1872, *Inconstant* went into reserve for eight years. There were two reasons why she was so treated. As the most expensive cruiser in existence it was cheaper to keep an armoured battleship in commission, while her speed made her an awkward squadron vessel. Under topsails alone, she was always over-running other ships, while her economical cruising speed under steam was sometimes better than the top speed of consorts. In 1880 she was employed taking relief crews to the Mediterranean and then became flagship of a new Detached Squadron bound away around the world. She rushed to Alexandria in 1882, but was too late to take part in the bombardment, and then went into reserve for twenty-two years. She was a gunnery hulk from 1904, and from 1920, as *Defence II*, was moored in the Hamoaze as part of the Devonport torpedo school, being broken up in 1956.

HMS INCONSTANT

HMS INFLEXIBLE

BATTLESHIP, LAUNCHED 1876, 320 FEET LONG, 11 880 TONS

Armament	Four 16-inch MLR guns and six 20-pounders. Two torpedo carriages and two submerged bow tubes. In 1885 the 20 pounders were changed to 4-inch BL guns, and in 1897 the 4-inch guns were replaced by 4.7-inch quickfirers.
Armour	16–24 inches amidships; 16–17 inches on turrets.
Designer	Nathaniel Barnaby.
Builder	Royal Dockyard, Portsmouth.
Horsepower	8407 Indicated Horsepower.
Speed	14.75 knots.
Scrapped	Sold out of the service in 1903.

The importance of *Inflexible* in design terms is that she was the supreme example of the citadel ship designed to take punishment. The central part of the ship was a huge coffer-dam protecting the engines, boilers and magazines and crowned with a pair of turrets set *en echelon*. The ends of the ship were unarmoured but a maze of cork-lined chambers surrounded the citadel itself. One consequence was that her first captain reported that men lost their way in this iron labyrinth and had to be guided by a colour-code painted on the bulkheads and passages. She had, it was universally agreed, the ugliest profile of any ship afloat. However, her size and gun-power caught the public imagination, while the public wrangling between her designer, Nathaniel Barnaby, and his brother-in-law, the former Chief Constructor Edward James Reed, made the ship just as much a sensation as in the *Dreadnought* debate a quarter of a century later.

Commissioned in 1881, *Inflexible* was in the Mediterranean in time to take part in the bombardment of Alexandria the following year. She fired 88 of her huge shells, and had two men killed in the vicinity of one of her unprotected 20-pounders. The real damage on board was done by the concussion of her own guns, which rent the upperworks and smashed her boats. She came back to Portsmouth for a refit and made the first change in secondary armament, and then set off for a second Mediterranean tour. After a spell as Portsmouth guardship, *Inflexible* went into reserve. She could only make 10½ knots at this stage in her life and went further downhill to dockyard reserve in 1901, being sold for breaking up in 1903.

HMS INFLEXIBLE

HMS IRIS

CRUISER, LAUNCHED 1877, 300 FEET LONG, 3735 TONS

Armament	Ten 64-pounder MLR guns at first and four torpedo carriages. Then, thirteen 5-inch BLR guns and four quickfirers.
Armour	No armour as such, but built wholly of steel and having numerous water-tight compartments.
Designers	Controller of the Navy. (Nathaniel Barnaby and William Henry White both claim to have played a leading part in the design.)
Builder	Pembroke Royal Dockyard.
Horsepower	7330 Indicated Horsepower.
Speed	18 knots.
Scrapped	Sold for breaking up in 1905.

This ship was destined always to be controversial. *Iris* was, with her sister *Mercury*, the fastest of her day. Nobody knew how to classify her. Nathaniel Barnaby insisted that she was an armed despatch vessel; Robinson, the Controller of the Navy, saw her as a fast cruiser protecting trade while Lord Gilford thought of her as an out-and-out commerce raider. Some years later it was decided to record her as a second-class cruiser, but the truth is that *Iris* was so far ahead of her time that she was employed, rather uselessly, as a despatch vessel because no-one had the imagination to create a role where her great speed could be exploited. Her place in the history of warship design rests on three salient points. Her hull form was followed by several generations of cruisers. The *Leander* class was a direct descendant of *Iris*, although there a knot of speed was sacrificed to accommodate an armoured deck. Finally, the argument that Britain could rely almost entirely on armed merchantmen in time of war and save money on warship construction was scuppered; Iris could have overtaken any vessel afloat in the late 1870s.

The ship was commissioned in 1880 and spent her early years in the Mediterranean. In 1882 she blockaded Damietta, while her men occupied Port Said. They were back in Port Said again in 1883 to put down local disturbances, and in 1884 formed part of Lord Charles Beresford's naval brigade that defended Suakin. *Iris*'s famous speed was down to a pedestrian 15 knots by 1898, and she slipped slowly down the reserve list until sold for breaking up in 1905.

HMS IRIS

HMS IRON DUKE

BATTLESHIP, LAUNCHED 1870, 280 FEET LONG, 6010 TONS

Armament	Ten 9-inch and four 6-inch MLR guns.
Armour	6–8 inches belt, 4–6 inches battery.
Designer	Edward James Reed.
Builder	Pembroke Royal Dockyard.
Horsepower	4830 Indicated Horsepower.
Speed	13.6 knots.
Scrapped	Sold in 1906 for breaking up.

Last of the 'Audacious' class of second-line battleships, she differed from her sisters, *Audacious*, *Invincible* and *Vanguard*, in having a hinged rather than a balanced rudder, which made her more manageable under sail. *Iron Duke* was one of the only group of vessels built from one design to emerge between the first use of armour in 1859 and the building of the 'Admiral' class early in the 1890s. The rest tended to be one-offs or half-sisters, for if one looks at, say, the armoured ships built in the 1860s, some thirteen are absolutely individual in design and only ten can be paired.

On commissioning, *Iron Duke* was briefly First Reserve Guardship before being selected as the new flagship of the China station. She was the first capital ship to use the Suez Canal, and on the way back grounded four times. She was destined to go aground rather often, being ashore on the Woosung bar in 1879 and having a too close acquaintance with Hokkaido the following year. Her most publicised accident was in 1875 when she rammed and sank *Vanguard* in fog off the Irish coast. An inexperienced officer in *Iron Duke* had altered course when the fog came down instead of following *Vanguard* directly, while the latter ship had to change course for a crossing sailing vessel and presented her beam to *Iron Duke's* ram. The wretched lieutenant deemed responsible was dismissed, and it was said that when he died of fever abroad a little while later the last words that passed his lips were 'Vanguard ahead . . . !'

The ship saw no active service and had a short life. She is chiefly remembered as the command of Vice-Admiral Charles Shadwell, a well-known eccentric and notable mathematician. His Star Tables were a standard work, and the Shadwell Prize was awarded each year to a general service officer who made the best amateur survey. After two tours in Chinese waters, and some spells on reserve at home, *Iron Duke* was sold for breaking up in 1906.

HMS IRON DUKE

HMS MEDINA

GUNBOAT, LAUNCHED 1876, 110 FEET LONG, 360 TONS

Armament	Three 64-pounder MLR guns.
Designers	Controller of the Navy, with under-water form suggested by Captain Trajano de Carvallo of the Brazilian Navy.
Builder	Palmer, Jarrow.
Horsepower	310 Indicated Horsepower.
Speed	9½ knots under engine; 5½ knots under canvas.
Scrapped	Sold out of the service at Bermuda in 1904.

Medina was the name-ship for a class of shallow-draught river gunboats, the others being *Dee, Don, Esk, Medway, Sabrina, Slaney, Spey, Tay, Tees, Trent* and *Tweed*. They were unarmoured, twin screw vessels with a draught of six feet, and *Medina*'s engines were by Hawthorn. The combination of shallow draught, short length and twin screws made them extremely manoeuvrable under power. Their sailing rig was a naval oddity, because the amount of canvas they carried was based on the allowance for gun-brigs – their distant ancestors in design terms – while it was disposed on three masts in the fashion of a barquentine. The official description of the rig was that the ships were three-masted brigantines.

Gunboats were popular with junior officers because they were the only class of armed ship that gave Lieutenants a chance of command. It was, of course, a rather more personal affair than in big ships, for with only about forty men in the crew it was often necessary for the captain to take the helm while practically everyone else manned the three guns. The two forward guns were at the break of the fo'c'sle and under the bowsprit. They had an arc of 80° from right ahead to almost on the beam, while the aft gun was positioned right over the rudder post.

Two years after she was built *Medina* was classified as non-seagoing, and at first she was employed locally at Portsmouth as a tender to *HMS Excellent*, the gunnery school. However, this did not prevent her being sent out to the West Indies where she served for a number of years. No note survives of her Atlantic passage, but as the voyage was the present-day equivalent of crossing in a Thames barge it must have been an exciting business. Stripped of her guns and hulked, she was eventually sold out of service at Bermuda in 1904.

HM GUN BOAT MEDINA

HMS MINOTAUR

BATTLESHIP, LAUNCHED 1863, 400 FEET LONG, 10 627 TONS

Armament	Four 9-inch guns and twenty-two 7-inch MLR guns initially, then seventeen 9-inch MLR guns.
Armour	5½ inches at sides tapering to 4½ inches at bow and stern.
Designer	Isaac Watts.
Builder	Thames Iron Works, Blackwall.
Horsepower	1350 Indicated Horsepower.
Speed	14.4 knots.
Scrapped	Broken up at Swansea in 1923.

A sister to *Agincourt*, *Minotaur* was designed by Isaac Watts who had a part in *Warrior*. *Minotaur* was an iron-hulled, five-masted, single-screw vessel with a rounded ram and reputed to be almost unmanageable under sail. She was cut down to a three-masted barque rig in 1893 when her active days were almost over. The ship had telescopic funnels, and as leader of the Channel Squadron would up-stage her lesser contemporaries by anchoring further off with the funnels down to get a good spot on the horizon. Five masts always looked impressive, and as an advertisement for the 'fleet in being' concept she was superb. Alas, she saw no action during a long career, being a day too late to take part in the attack on Alexandria.

Her original name was to have been *Elephant,* which might have been very appropriate because her one outstanding weakness as a warship was that she had a small radius of action. Her Penn's trunk engine was a prodigious user of coal, and even under the most favourable conditions – plain sail, port stunsails, a clean bottom, disconnected propellor and a Force 5–6 wind on the quarter – she could not manage more than 9½ knots under canvas. She was also slow in getting into service, for some years were spent altering rig and armament so that she did not start her career until four years after launching.

Minotaur was 18 years in commission, and was then 6 years in reserve before becoming a kind of laundry ship where hammocks were scrubbed. In 1918, as *Ganges II,* she flew the flag of the Rear-Admiral in charge of training, but in 1922 was sold for breaking up.

HMS MINOTAUR

HMS MONARCH

BATTLESHIP, LAUNCHED 1868, 330 FEET LONG, 8322 TONS

Armament	Four 12-inch MLR guns and three 7-inch MLR guns. Two of the latter subsequently changed for 9-inch guns.
Armour	Sides 7-inch decreasing to 4-inch; turrets had 9-inch to 10-inch armour.
Designer	Chief Constructor's Department, Admiralty.
Builder	Royal Dockyard, Chatham.
Horsepower	1100.
Speed	13½ knots.
Scrapped	Broken up in 1905.

Monarch was the first blue-water turret ship and was, in a very real sense, the prototype for the kind of battleship that made up the bulk of the fleet in World War One. She had steam-powered steering and rotating turrets, carried her main armament outside the hull and on the centre line and fired shells through rifled barrels. She had a balanced rudder, was a buoyant seaboat and a steady gun platform. Her upper masts were sent down when she cleared for action, and with a crew of over 500 men this drill took 8 to 10 minutes. In a word, *Monarch* was what Cowper Coles was aiming for with the design of *Captain*, and although he always denied having any part in the design of the former ship the Admiralty paid him the tribute of saying that both vessels owed much to his 'highly practical, inventive and ingenious mind'. Our summing-up of the design controversy of the 1860s may be that Cowper Coles was right to stress the primacy of the revolving turret, but wrong to cling to reduced freeboard. He had, perhaps, not fully digested the lesson of Ericsson's *Monitor*. It had defeated a heavily-armoured broadside ship, but had then foundered on meeting a gale of wind.

Monarch served in the Channel Squadron and in the Mediterranean and had two moments of fame. Shortly after commissioning she had the unusual duty of taking the remains of George Peabody (renowned as a philanthropist and a builder of cheap housing for the poor) to his native land. The Americans were most impressed with a turret ship that could cross the Atlantic, and crowds flocked to see her. In 1882 she was one of eight ships to bombard Alexandria, firing 125 rounds at shore targets.

In 1897 she was sent to Simonstown as a guardship with a half-complement, and reduced to being a depot ship under the name *Simoom* in 1904. She was sold for scrap in 1905 after a useful career of 26 years in commission.

HMS MONARCH

HMS NEPTUNE

BATTLESHIP, LAUNCHED 1878, 300 FEET LONG, 9310 TONS

Armament	Four 12-inch guns and two 9-inch MLR guns (see text for changes).
Armour	9–12 inches belt, 11–13 inches on turrets.
Designer	Edward James Reed.
Builder	J. & W. Dudgeon, Millwall.
Horsepower	7993 Indicated Horsepower.
Speed	14.2 knots.
Scrapped	Broken up in Holland in 1904.

This ship began life as the Brazilian *Independencia* and was purchased by the British Government in 1878 at a time when war with Russia seemed imminent. The Brazilians had wanted a 'rigged *Devastation*', and Reed had shrugged his shoulders at the incongruity and got on with the job. When the British exercised their right of emergency purchase they paid about twice what '*Devastation*' had cost and got a strange bargain for their pains.

It had been intended to arm *Independencia* with four 12-inch and two 8-inch BL guns, but these were replaced by standard Navy 12-inch and 9-inch MLR weapons. The remaining armament changed twice — from 20-pounders to Nordenfelts to fourteen 3-pounder and 6-pounder quickfirers. Two 14-inch torpedo tubes, one each side, were also fitted. The *Independencia* had been barque-rigged with double topsails on the merchant ship pattern, but greater crew numbers, and the strength of tradition, caused a change to single topsails. When the mainmast – which was too near the funnel – got smoke-corroded the ship was sailed under fore and mizen only; a rig that was only suitable, according to seamen, for 'anging around Wapping High Street'. Her engines were the last set of Penn trunk engines used in a warship, and were prodigious users of coal. Her best feature was the ample accommodation under the poop designed for a Brazilian admiral and his staff, and as she was never a flagship the wardroom officers had the benefit of ample room, and the first bathroom seen in the fleet.

Commissioned in 1883 for Channel service, she transferred to the Mediterranean in 1885 and had the task of escorting *Monarch* back to base when the latter had trouble with the stern tube liners. Back at Portsmouth in 1886, she was fitted with military rig, machine guns and a net defence, and was thereafter a coastguard ship at Holyhead and in reserve. Always a clumsy ship, she blundered out of history in appropriate style, colliding with *Victory* as she was towed away to the breakers.

HMS NEPTUNE

HMS NORTHUMBERLAND

BATTLESHIP, LAUNCHED 1866, 400 FEET LONG, 10584 TONS

Armament	Four 9-inch MLR guns and twenty-two 8-inch and two 7-inch MLR guns initially. Later, in 1875, seven 9-inch MLR guns and twenty 8-inch MLR guns.
Armour	Sides – 5½ inches.
Builder	Mare, Millwall.
Horsepower	1350.
Speed	14.1 knots.
Scrapped	Broken up in 1935.

Similar to *Minotaur*, she was about half a knot slower under power and rather more than that under sail when compared to the other five-masters. She drew more aft, and could scarcely make seven knots under sail in the most favourable conditions. Cut down to barque rig in 1875, there was no improvement in performance.

Northumberland was a long time launching, being stuck on the ways for a month, and then a long time fitting-out because her builders went into liquidation. Ready for service in 1868 under that notable naval character, Captain Roderick Dew, she took part in the tow of the Bermuda Floating Dock to Madeira, and was next in the news in 1872 when her cable failed – not for the first time – so that she fell across the bows of *Hercules* and was impaled on the latter's ram before drifting clear. In 1875 she had an extensive re-fit when new armament was put into her.

For four years *Northumberland* was in dockyard hands, but on being re-commissioned in 1879 she had two spells in the Channel Squadron, having a minor part in the Egyptian campaign of 1882. Transferred to the reserve in 1890, she was down-graded to harbour service a year later. However, this was not the end, for she became a training school for stokers at Chatham under the name *Acheron*. Next, she went further down the list to be coal hulk C.8 at Invergordon, being renumbered C.68 in 1927. Sold for breaking in that year, there was a reprieve when she was sold for further service as a hulk at Dakar under the name *Stedmound*. Finally, in 1935, she was sold for breaking up. *Minotaur*, one of the other five-masters, had gone 12 years before; *Agincourt* would survive another 25 years.

HMS NORTHUMBERLAND

HMS ORONTES

TROOPSHIP, LAUNCHED 1862, 350 FEET LONG, 5600 TONS

Armament	Three 4-pounder guns.
Designer	Controller of the Navy.
Builder	Lairds, Birkenhead.
Horsepower	2600 Indicated Horsepower.
Speed	13 knots.
Scrapped	Sold in 1893 for breaking up on the Thames.

An iron screw steamer, *Orontes* was originally 300 feet long and displaced 4857 tons, but in 1875 she was re-built to make her fifty feet longer and the displacement tonnage went up to 5600. Compound engines were installed at the re-building. Whereas the *Crocodile* and her sisters were primarily Indian troopers, *Orontes* often carried men across the Atlantic and to South Africa. The naval association was much stronger in that, for example, her captain in 1885, Hilary Andoe, was awarded the CB for his work as transport officer ashore at Suakin and Trinkita. No such opportunities were available to officers serving in the Indian troopers, who tended to plough monotonously too and fro between Bombay and Portsmouth without much contact with the fleet, and there was a general impression that appointments to troopers went only to the old, the incompetent or the eccentric. The ships were known as 'lobster pots' because they carried soldiers, and problems were always arising because the Army loathed being subject to naval discipline. Worst of all from the wardroom point of view, the popular belief was that there was no promotion to be found in troopers.

Orontes had two moments of 'media attention' in her long life. In 1879 she was selected to bring back to England the body of the Prince Imperial, Empress Eugenie's son, who had been killed in South Africa, and for that voyage she was painted slate grey instead of the usual white. At the Spithead Review of 1887 she was rammed by the Royal Yacht *Victoria and Albert*, to the great embarrassment of the monarch and the Admiralty as the Crown Prince of Germany, later Kaiser Wilhelm II was present. She was coming to the end of her useful life anyway, and was sold for breaking up in 1893.

HMS ORONTES

HMS RALEIGH

FRIGATE, LAUNCHED 1873, 298 FEET LONG, 5200 TONS

Armament	Two 9-inch, fourteen 7-inch and six 64-pounder ML guns initially, but after ten years changed to eight 7-inch, eight 6-inch and eight 5-inch guns, plus two Whitehead torpedo carriages.
Designer	Edward James Reed.
Builder	Royal Dockyard, Chatham.
Horsepower	6158 Indicated Horsepower.
Speed	15½ knots.
Scrapped	Broken up in 1905.

Her first commanding officer was George Tryon, later to lose his life in the *Victoria* while Commander-in-Chief in the Mediterranean. Tryon had private means, and her launch was the largest rowing boat in the Royal Navy, some 50 feet long and propelled by 22 oars in place of the usual 18. A descendant of *Inconstant*, she was a large unarmoured frigate fit to do the work of a colonial cruiser, and it is recorded that she passed Cape Horn under canvas on her second commission, being the last frigate to do so.

From 1884 to 1895 *Raleigh* served as flagship of the Cape of Good Hope and West Africa station, and her crew was frequently employed ashore in punitive actions. On one occasion her first lieutenant, a Royal Marine officer and a number of seamen were killed in a skirmish up the the Gambia River. When she came back to home waters there was a further lease of life as the commodore's ship in the Training Squadron. In 1899 she led the last squadron of naval ships to put to sea under canvas, and the event was immortalised in a Harold Wyllie painting. *Raleigh* was dismantled in 1899, spent six years in reserve and was broken up in 1905.

She was an excellent seaboat, and had the longest commissioned overseas service of any mid-Victorian major warship, spending nineteen years on foreign stations. She also bore one of the finest figureheads of the portrait type. Sir Walter appeared in half-length and more than double life-size. He was seven feet from head to waist, and was supported on wings spread wide and bearing the unmistakeable leaves of the tobacco and potato plants. The Americans had a vessel of the same name, but pronounciation soon showed which ship was being referred to. Theirs was 'Rallee'; the British ship was 'Rawley'.

HMS RALEIGH

HMS ROYAL ALFRED

BATTLESHIP, LAUNCHED 1864, 373 FEET LONG, 6707 TONS

Armament	Ten 9-inch MLR guns and eight 7-inch MLR guns.
Armour	The timber sides of the ship were a maximum of 29$\frac{1}{2}$ inches thick, while the thickest portion of the added armour was 6 inches. Generally, it was 4$\frac{1}{2}$ inches thick.
Designer	Edward James Reed.
Builder	Royal Dockyard, Portsmouth.
Horsepower	8000.
Speed	12.4 knots.
Scrapped	Sold for breaking up in 1885.

Royal Alfred was intended to be a ninety-one gun, two-decked line-of-battle ship, but although laid down in 1859 she was five years on the stocks as the lessons learned when putting engines and armour into the *Prince Consort* and *Royal Oak* were digested. *Royal Alfred* was the last major wooden warship built at Portsmouth. She was ship-rigged and an excellent performer under sail, once making 12$\frac{1}{2}$ knots in a full gale with close-reefed fore and main topsails and single reef in the foresail. This was slight improvement on her best speed under engine.

The delay in building and fitting her out meant that she could be provided with the new 9-inch guns, and the armament was never changed. In 1867 she went as flagship on the North America station, showing the flag from Labrador to Trinidad during two long commissions. She grounded once on the Bahama Bank, but otherwise her service was uneventful. Paid off in 1874, *Royal Alfred* went into reserve at Portland. Surveys showed that her hull was sound but the boiler pressure was poor through corrosion and new boilers were needed. The Admiralty prevaricated for some time and finally disposed of her in 1885.

Given her history, it seems that *Royal Alfred* was predestined for early obsolescence. When she was built it had been a matter of using up half-constructed wooden hulls, cladding them with armour plate, cutting down top hamper, altering the length and putting in the new 9-inch guns. Her Maudslay engine of 800 nominal horsepower with six boilers and hoisting propellor was that designed for an unarmoured ship, and it is proper to think of her as the imperfect hybrid exactly half way between the wooden wall and the ironclad.

HMS ROYAL ALFRED

HMS SHAH

FRIGATE, LAUNCHED 1873, 335 FEET LONG, 6250 TONS

Armament	Two 9-inch, sixteen 7-inch and eight 6-inch MLR guns with two 16-inch torpedo carriages.
Horsepower	7477 Indicated Horsepower.
Speed	16.45 knots under steam; 13.2 knots under sail.
Scrapped	Sold for breaking at Bermuda in 1919.

Originally to be named *Blonde*, this ship was called *Shah* as a compliment to Persia and was the largest square-rigged iron vessel without armour launched in Britain. Classified as a frigate, it is best to think of her as a first-class colonial cruiser with two claims to fame. She fought a single-ship action in an age when such opportunities were rare, while dockyard tradition has it that her masts became *Victory*'s lower masts during an early twentieth-century restoration.

Shah had only one commission, but it was crammed with incident. In 1876, as Pacific flagship, the problem facing Rear-Admiral De Horsey was one of politics and piracy. A Presidential candidate in Peru, Don Pierola, had taken over the armoured turret ship *Huascar* and was seizing coal from British ships. *Shah* and the corvette *Amethyst* tracked down the *Huascar*. Admiral De Horsey demanded that Don Pierola surrender for judgement on acts of piracy, but 'President' Pierola repudiated the charge because it had been an act of government and lawful. The *Huascar* set off for the shelter of the land; *Shah* gave chase and opened fire. The Peruvian vessel was hit repeatedly, but sustained little internal damage because of her armour, while *Shah* was only cut about the rigging. *Huascar* steamed along the shore to Iquique and surrendered to the 'official' Peruvian Navy under Commodore More, an Irish officer.

Pierola became a national hero, and his political opponent, the 'official' President, recognised a winner when he saw one and joined in the demand for compensation. The upshot was that *Shah* was ordered home and De Horsey received no further advancement. On the way back, *Shah* was diverted to Natal to land 400 officers, seamen and marines who fought ashore for five months as an infantry battalion. The ship was tinged with the disapproval that the Admiral had to endure, and she was first a depot ship in Bermuda, then a coal hulk, and was scrapped in 1919. The very last sailing frigate had a short but eventful life, being probably the last unarmoured ship to give an armoured vessel a trouncing.

HMS SHAH & CHILLIAN SHIP 'HUASCAR'

HMS SHANNON

CRUISER, LAUNCHED 1875, 260 FEET LONG, 5670 TONS

Armament	Two 10-inch and seven 9-inch MLR guns.
Armour	A belt of 6–9 inches along the waterline, except for 60 feet at the bows, and 1½ inches protecting magazines, machinery and steering gear.
Designer	Nathaniel Barnaby.
Builder	Pembroke Royal Dockyard.
Horsepower	3370 Indicated Horsepower.
Speed	12.3 knots.
Scrapped	Sold for breaking up in 1899.

This is the first ship to which the appellation of 'armoured cruiser' may be said to apply, although she was officially classified as a second-class battleship. The truth is that *Shannon* was too weakly-armed to be a battleship, and too slow to be a cruiser, and of 21 years of service only three were passed on foreign stations. For the rest, she was either a coastguard ship, on reserve or under repair.

Barnaby, her designer, seems to have failed with *Shannon* because of an inability to see that cruisers were not just small ironclads. His political masters were undoubtedly influenced by some Russian designs when the ship was ordered, and they were keen to get a counter on the board to block a suspected move. Nobody seems to have appreciated that the first requirement of such a ship was speed, despite the fact that the developing compound engine could confer such an essential advantage. She was, it is true, given a full ship rig, but was cut down to a barque in 1876. There were no stunsails, and her record is one of a poor sailer.

Shannon went out to China in 1877, but was soon back for alterations. Her next lengthy tour abroad was in 1879 when she went to the Pacific for two years. Four torpedo tubes and a few machine guns were added to her armament at the 1881 refit, and in 1883 she became a tender to *Warrior* at Portsmouth. She served at Greenock and Bantry Bay as a coastguard ship, then went into reserve and was sold for breaking up in 1899. The kindest thing one can say about *Shannon* is that the lessons learned in her building were put into good effect when *Nelson* and *Northampton* followed her off the blocks a year later.

HMS SHANNON

HMS SULTAN

BATTLESHIP, LAUNCHED 1870, 325 FEET LONG, 9540 TONS

Armament	Eight 10-inch and four 9-inch MLR guns (see text for later additions).
Armour	6–9 inches belt, 1½ inches skin. 8–9 inches on the battery.
Designer	Edward James Reed.
Builder	Royal Dockyard, Chatham.
Horsepower	7720 Indicated Horsepower.
Speed	14.1 knots.
Scrapped	Sold for breaking up in 1946

Sultan was ordered at a time when the vices and virtues of turret ships had yet to be fully explored, and consequently her armament was of the broadside type in an armoured central battery on the *Hercules* pattern. When she was 9 years old her armament was increased by the addition of four torpedo carriages and seven 4-inch BL guns, while in the 1890s *Sultan* was fitted with another four 4.7-inch quick-firers on the upper deck amidships. Ship-rigged at first, she was cut down to a barque in 1876 and to military rig in the 1890s.

She was with the Channel Squadron for her maiden commission, and in 1876 went to the Mediterranean under the command of the Duke of Edinburgh, Queen Victoria's second son. *Sultan* took part in Phipps Hornby's show of strength off Constantinople when Russian troops were on the outskirts of the city, and was one of eight armoured vessels involved in the bombardment of Alexandria in 1882. Although much battered by enemy fire, only two men were killed and eight injured when a projectile hit the unarmoured battery under the topgallant fo'c'sle. The most dramatic episode of her career took place in 1889 when she struck an uncharted rock in the South Comino Channel off Malta and slowly sank in eight fathoms of water after *Temeraire* had vainly tried to pull her off. An Italian salvage firm raised her for £50 000, and then a further £200 000 was spent on 'modernisation' between 1893 and 1896.

Oscar Parkes' comment that 'the old ship was never worth it' best sums up this gross Admiralty error, for although new triple-expansion engines and quick-firing guns were put in there was no disguising the fact that the *Sultan* was hopelessly obsolete. In 1906 she became an artificers training ship as *Fisgard IV*, and then a floating repair workshop. At the outbreak of World War Two she had an extra lease of life as a depot ship for Portsmouth-based minesweepers, but in 1946 was finally sold for scrap.

HMS SULTAN

HMS TEMERAIRE

BATTLESHIP, LAUNCHED 1876, 285 FEET LONG, 8415 TONS

Armament	Four 11-inch MLR and four 10-inch MLR guns (see text for later additions).
Armour	8–11 inches amidships
Designer	Committee on Designs, Admiralty
Builder	Royal Dockyard, Chatham.
Horsepower	7516 Indicated Horsepower.
Speed	14.6 knots.
Scrapped	Sold for to a Dutch shipbreaker in 1921.

The biggest two-masted warship capable of being propelled by sail alone, *Temeraire* had the largest foresail set square and the largest main trysail set fore-and-aft ever made. She was consequently known as 'The Great Brig' and her armament reflected the same kind of uncertain compromise that had failed to give priority to one of two means of propulsion. Some of her guns were in upper-deck, centre-line turrets, while the rest were broadside guns as in the *Alexandra*, a near-contemporary. Additionally, the Admiralty had taken the opportunity of trying out an idea borrowed from land fortresses of keeping guns in shelter pits until they were needed. The machinery involved was named after its developer as Montcrieff's Disappearing Carriage.

The sunken armoured pits in which the guns went up and down were called barbettes, and hydraulic pressure worked the machinery. An armoured trunk went down into the hull and carried the ammunition hoist. There were only two snags. The weight was crippling and there was no defence against plunging fire. In the event, *Temeraire* remained the only ship to be equipped in this way, although the Montcrieff system was widely used for shore batteries. At completion it was realised that there was no provision for defence against torpedoes, and she received four additional 20-pounder guns, later replaced by six 4-inch guns, two torpedo carriages and a pair of 30-inch searchlights. Strangely enough, the power for the last-named was not employed for internal lighting and the crew used candles below decks.

After commissioning, *Temeraire* served all her time but a few months in the Mediterranean, going up to Constantinople in a show of strength in 1878 and being one of eight ships bombarding Alexandria in 1882. In 1890 she tacked to an anchorage at Suda Bay under sail alone – the last British battleship to perform the feat. Relegated to the reserve in 1881, she became *Indus II* in 1904 and the school ship *Akbar* in 1915, being sold for scrap in 1921.

HMS TEMERAIRE

HMS TRAFALGAR

BATTLESHIP, LAUNCHED 1841, 216 FEET LONG, 2900 TONS

Armament	120 SB guns, mostly 32-pounders. Later reduced to twenty-four guns.
Designer	William Rule.
Builder	Royal Dockyard, Woolwich.
Horsepower	500.
Speed	10.9 knots.
Scrapped	Broken up in 1906.

This two-decker was 11½ years on the stocks, and her first five commissions were under sail alone. She was, however, a dull performer, for when in her prime in 1847 and serving with the Channel Fleet she took part in a sailing trial over a 30-mile course off Lisbon. She was not mentioned among the first ships home. At the outbreak of the Crimean War *Trafalgar* was part of the fleet assembled in the Black Sea, and she both bombarded Sebastapol and sent men ashore with her 32-pounders to join the siege of the city. Her lack of auxiliary power was noted, and in 1859 a set of Maudslay engines driving a single screw were installed.

It cannot be said that her engines were very successful, for when Henry Molesworth joined her in 1870 he reported that they were so corroded that a stoker pushed his slice through the crown of the firebox, while her old-fashioned square boilers could hold a head of steam of from only four to seven pounds. He was laconic about her speed. Under engines, he said, *Trafalgar* could make about three knots, but only with the wind aft. She steered by hand, and in bad weather relieving tackles were clapped on and manned by twenty men – ten each side. She was a lively ship, and on occasion the round shot would jump out of the lockers and roll about the decks so as to injure anyone who could not leap out of the way.

The last two-decker in commission, she was renamed *Boscawen* in 1873 and employed as a training ship at Portland. She remained there until 1905 when the training establishment was closed down, and was broken up the following year. She had 13 captains prior to 1871, and with her later commanding officers as a training ship it is said that she was the only warship, save *Victory*, to have had a score of captains between launching and being laid up.

HMS TRAFALGAR

HMS TURQUOISE

CORVETTE, LAUNCHED 1876, 220 FEET LONG, 2120 TONS

Armament	Twelve 64-pounder MLR guns.
Designer	Admiralty.
Builder	Earle, Hull.
Horsepower	1990 Indicated Horsepower.
Speed	12.3 knots.
Scrapped	Sold out of the service in 1892.

The class of six iron and timber composite ships laid down in 1875 comprise the sisters *Emerald* (whose name is usually taken as that of the class), *Ruby*, *Opal*, *Garnet*, *Turquoise* and *Tourmaline*, and they were designed to have a displacement tonnage of 1870. Forty tons of ballast had to be put in the hulls to improve sailing performance, and the displacement figure for *Turquoise* was 2120 tons. Conventionally armed with muzzle-loading 64-pounders, she was, like her sisters, rather too slow to do effective duty as a colonial cruiser. She went out to the Pacific in 1877, and on return was cut down to a barque and dispatched to the East Indies. She came home after 7 years, but was deemed unfit for conversion or further service and was sold for breaking up in 1892.

Turquoise's two commissions in the Indian Ocean were typical of the police role assigned to ships of her type in the period. In 1885, for example, her captain was ordered to Rangoon where his instructions were to form a naval brigade to help the Indian government capture Mandalay, depose King Thibaw and put down the dacoits. His motley flotilla was made up of paddle steamers, launches and barges fitted with two of *Turquoise's* 64-pounders as improvised gunboats. Robert Woodward's fleet destroyed a battery of eleven guns near Pagan, and another fortified camp at Mingyan was subdued. His boats anchored off Yandabo where a treaty had ended the Burma War of 1826, and eventually reached Mandalay. Some of *Turquoise's* crew got as far as Bhamo near the Chinese frontier in a small steamer. Woodward was awarded the CB for his part in the successful end to what historians have come to call the Third Burma War.

In 1887 *Turquoise* was cruising in search of slavers off the East African coast when her pinnace, under Lieutenant Fogerty Fegan, engaged a dhow. Fierce hand-to-hand fighting ensued. Lieutenant Fegen killed two Arabs with his revolver and ran a third through with his sword. The slaving dhow beached itself after its helmsman was killed with a rifle shot, and the much-battered boats' crew succeeded in rescuing 53 slaves.

HMS TURQUOISE

The Royal Yacht
VICTORIA AND ALBERT

ROYAL YACHT, LAUNCHED 1855, 338 FEET LONG, 2345 TONS

Armament	Two light guns for signalling purposes.
Designer	Surveyor's Department, Admiralty.
Builder	Pembroke Royal Dockyard.
Horsepower	600.
Speed	18 knots.
Scrapped	Broken up at Portsmouth in 1904.

A wooden paddler, laid down as the *Windsor Castle*, this vessel succeeded another Royal Yacht of the same name which was then called *Osborne*. The ship depicted opposite had lofty masts for the display of oversize ensigns and had the traditional black hull with a gold riband still employed for today's *Britannia*. The seamen employed aboard were called 'riggers', and the marines wore a special white drill uniform to match the whites of the Navy men in summer. Soft shoes were worn when the sovereign was aboard, and many orders were given by signs to keep the noise down.

The ship was used almost exclusively for ceremonial purposes, and in particular would convey Queen Victoria and her guests through the fleet at Royal reviews. The principal reviews of the reign were in 1856, 1887 and 1897. The first-named was to honour the 240 ships that had served in the Crimea and Baltic, and about half of these were gun vessels and gunboats. The 1887 review was a more controversial affair because it was marred by a number of collisions. *Black Prince* struck *Agincourt*, *Ajax* hit *Devastation* and *Victoria and Albert* collided with the troopship *Orontes*. The Crown Prince and Princess of Germany were present, and the *Daily News* commented that 'foreign visitors should be kept out of the way until our bumping races of ironclads have come to an end'. Edward James Reed, former Chief Constructor and now a Member of Parliament, observed that only six or seven of the review ships were fit to go to war. The 1897 review on the monarch's Diamond Jubilee was better managed, but journalists noted that many old ships armed with muzzle-loaders had been brought out of reserve to swell the numbers.

Comfortable and imposing, *Victoria and Albert* retained her position until 1900 although a third ship of the name had been made ready the year before. She was finally broken up in 1904.

THE ROYAL YACHT VICTORIA AND ALBERT

HMS VICTORY

BATTLESHIP, LAUNCHED 1765, 226 FEET LONG, 3500 TONS

Armament	Thirty 32-pounders, twenty-eight 24-pounders, forty-four 12-pounders and two 68-pound carronades.
Designer	Thomas Slade.
Builder	Royal Dockyard, Chatham.
Location	In dry dock at Portsmouth Naval Base.

From the seventeeth-century it was the custom to classify warships by the number of their guns, and *Victory* is a first-rate line-of-battle ship because she carried over a hundred guns. Between 1812 and 1817 the number of guns fell to 98, so that technically she was briefly a second-rate. The keel of 20-inch square teak was laid down at Chatham in 1759, and the ship used up 300 000 cubic feet of timber in the building. As is so often the case, a weapon built for one war (in *Victory*'s case the Seven Years War) was too long in the making to influence it, for the ship was a couple of years late for that conflict, and was laid up, not being commissioned until 1778.

Victory was, in turn, the flagship of Augustus Keppel, Richard Kempenfelt, Lord Howe, Lord Hood and Sir John Jervis. Nelson hoisted his flag in her in 1803, and two and a half years later she bore his body back to England after Trafalgar. She was paid off in 1812 for harbour service, was the flagship, a receiving ship and the flagship again from 1891 to the present day. In 1921 Lord Milford Haven, first President of the Society for Nautical Research, called for the preservation of the old ship and her restoration to Trafalgar condition and appearance. In the following year she was put into dry dock at Portsmouth, and ten years of intensive work followed financed by the Save the Victory Fund. She is still a serving ship, manned by officers and men of the Royal Navy, and at the time of writing visitors are shown round by seamen of her complement. Passing warships pay their compliments to the old three-decker, and her White Ensign flies high over the dockyard buildings that surround her. *Victory* was an old ship when Victoria came to the throne: she has seen the Coronation of eight monarchs and should, God willing, see as many more come to reign.

HMS VICTORY

HMS VOLAGE

CORVETTE, LAUNCHED 1869, 270 FEET LONG, 3320 TONS

Armament	At first, six 7-inch MLR and four 6-inch MLR guns. Then carried eighteen 6-inch MLR guns, and finally fitted with ten 6-inch BLR and two 6-inch MLR guns.
Designer	Controller of the Navy.
Builder	Thames Shipbuilding Company, Blackwall.
Horsepower	600.
Speed	15 knots steam; 13 knots sail.
Scrapped	Sold for breaking up in 1904.

Volage derived from the *Inconstant* design, but was smaller and less heavily-gunned. Her characteristics were speed combined with seakeeping qualities, an upper-deck broadside armament and an iron hull planked with oak and copper-sheathed for long spells at sea without dockyard attention. She was briefly with the Channel Squadron on being commissioned, but in late 1870 joined the Detached or Flying Squadron on a round-the-world voyage showing the flag. In 1874 *Volage* had a more demanding solo role, being chosen to take a party of scientists to Kerguelen in the remotest part of the South Indian Ocean to observe the transit of Venus. While there, she made her own discovery of the previously uncharted Volage Shoal by bumping over it and leaving some part of her oak planking behind. The general success of *Volage* led the Admiralty to build *Rover* – a slightly heavier ship – in 1874.

She next went as senior officer's ship on the South American station, being usually based at Rio de Janeiro, and came home in 1879 for re-fit, new boilers and a rearmament. In 1885 she joined her sister ship *Active* in the Training Squadron, and this very graceful pair covered many thousands of sea miles together until the squadron was disbanded in 1899. Known to the seamen as 'Vollidge', she was immensely popular and very handy at tacking and wearing ship under sail. Her fine lines forward made her a somewhat wet ship, and she was not a stable gun platform in anything of a head sea, but that was compensated for by her excellent accommodation as the main armament was on the upper deck and did not intrude into living space. She was put in reserve for a short time after the demise of the Training Squadron, and was sold for breaking up in 1904.

HMS VOLAGE

HMS WARRIOR

BATTLESHIP, LAUNCHED 1860, 380 FEET LONG, 9137 TONS

Armament	Originally, eleven 100-pounder SB Armstrong guns, twenty-six SBML 68-pounders and four SB 40-pounder guns. Four 8-inch MLR and twenty-eight 7-inch MLR guns fitted after 1867.
Armour	Sides 4½ inches over 208 feet of the central part of the hull.
Designers	Scott Russell and Isaac Watts.
Builder	Mare, Blackwall.
Horsepower	1250.
Speed	14.3 knots; 13 knots under canvas.
Location	Still afloat as a museum ship at Portsmouth.

Warrior was the first major armoured warship to be built wholly of iron, and its construction was viewed at the time as a risky gamble. When the First Lord of the Admiralty confided to the builder that he wondered how he had mustered up enough courage to place the order the latter retorted that he too had often wondered how he had gathered up enough courage to carry out the task. There were four major innovations involved. Armour plate had earlier been added to wooden hulls to make the 'floating batteries' of the Crimea War, but it was now an integral part of a fast warship. Internal sub-divisions safeguarded flotation in the event of damage, while frame and shell were of iron. Finally, her length was six and a half times the beam – she was over a hundred feet longer than the largest three-decker in service.

Warrior served two commissions in the Channel Squadron, and with her sister ship *Black Prince* took part in the epic deep-sea tow of the Bermuda Floating Dock from Porto Santo to Bermuda in 1869. In 1875 she became the Portland guardship, transferring to the the Clyde as the coastguard ship after 6 years. She went into reserve in 1884, but in 1904 had a further lease of life as an auxiliary workshop hulk under the name of *Vernon II*. Periodic surveys showed that the iron work was sound, and her next duty was as hulk C.77 at Pembroke Dock. Her importance as the ancestor of the British armoured fleet was eventually recognised, and after extensive renovation on the north-east coast she took up her present berth as a museum ship in Portsmouth in 1987.

HMS WARRIOR

HMS WILD SWAN

SLOOP, LAUNCHED 1876, 170 FEET LONG, 1130 TONS.

Armament	Two 7-inch and four 64-pounder MLR guns at first, then two 6-inch and six 5-inch BLR guns.
Designer	Nathaniel Barnaby.
Builder	Napier, Glasgow.
Horsepower	1090 Indicated Horsepower after the refit of 1881–84.
Speed	11.35 knots under engine; 10 knots under canvas.
Scrapped	Sold in 1920 for breaking up.

A composite ship built chiefly of iron and teak, *Wild Swan* was one of a class which included *Penguin, Osprey, Pelican* and *Cormorant*. Her guns were originally ranged two a side and one at bow and stern, increased to three a side after 1884. She was barque-rigged, and had a total sail area, excluding stunsails, of 14 800 square feet.

Commissioned in 1877 for the East Indies station, *Wild Swan* spent long periods on anti-slavery patrols, and an incident in 1880 off the coast of Mozambique highlights a facet of naval life that has received little attention from historians. Many ships on foreign stations are permitted to engage temporary crew-men for a single commission, and the brave conduct of a locally engaged Arab seaman was accorded rare official acknowledgement. A rescued slave called Farejallah fell overboard and was attacked by a shark. The Seedie Tindal – bosun's mate – promptly jumped in after him and got him back aboard, although the victim soon died. The name of the Seedie Tindal of the *Wild Swan* was Farabani, and he was awarded the Albert Medal for saving life at sea.

Wild Swan was given new machinery and guns in the refit of 1881–84, and there followed two commissions in the Pacific. When the ship came home in 1898 she went into Third-Class Reserve, but in 1904 was sent round to Aberdeen to be the Royal Naval Reserve drill ship. She replaced the old frigate *Clyde*, and took her name. In 1913 the ship moved on to Rosyth as a base ship, and during the First World War was a depot ship for destroyers with the name of *Columbine*. Her teak and iron construction had made for a relatively long life, but in 1920 with a reduction in the work centred on Rosyth she was sold for breaking up.

HMS WILD SWAN

BIBLIOGRAPHY

Archibald, E.H.H. *The Fighting Ship in the Royal Navy*, 1984.

Ballard, G.A., *The Black Battlefleet*, 1980.

Bedford, F.G.D., *The Sailor's Pocket Book*, 1885.

Callender, Geoffrey, *The Navy Side of British History*, 1924.

Chambers, B.M., *Salt Junk*, 1927.

Clowes, W.L., *The Royal Navy*, 1902

Colledge, J.J. *British Sailing Warships*, 1964.

Colledge, J.J., *Ships of the Royal Navy*, Newton Abbott, 1969.

Dawson, Christopher, *A Quest for Speed at Sea*, 1972.

Hayward, R., *The Story and Scandal of HMS Megaera*, Buxton, 1978.

Holmes, F.M., *England's Navy*, 1896.

Hough, Richard, *Man O'War*, 1979.

Kennedy, William, *Hurrah for the Life of a Sailor!*, 1900.

Lambert, A., *Battleships in Transition*, 1984.

Linklater, Eric, *The Voyage of the Challenger*, 1872.

Moseley, H.N., *Notes by a Naturalist made during the Voyage of HMS Challenger round the world in the years 1872-1876*. First published in 1879: new edition in 1944.

Parkes, Oscar, *British Battleships*, 1970 edition.

Price, Harry, *The Royal Tour*, 1901, Exeter, 1980.

Rogers, H.C.B. *Troopships and their History*, 1979 edition.

Schofield, B.B., *British Sea Power*, 1967.

Spratt, H.P., *Science Museum Handbook of the Collections illustrating Marine Engineering*, HMSO, 1953.

Trotter, W.P., *The Royal Navy in Old Photographs*, 1975.

White, C., *Victoria's Navy*, 1981 and 1983.

Williams, Hamilton, *Britain's Naval Power*, 1904.

Winton, John, *Hurrah for the Life of a Sailor!*, 1977.

Conway's All the World's Fighting Ships, 1860-1905, 1979.

Talbot Booth's All the World's Fighting Fleets, 1938.

Brassey's Naval Annual.

Jane's Fighting Ships.

The Mariner's Mirror.

Sea Breezes.

THE SOCIETY FOR NAUTICAL RESEARCH
Founded 1910

Patron
HRH The Duke of Edinburgh, KG, KT

The Society was founded in 1910 to encourage research into matters relating to seafaring and shipbuilding in all ages and among all nations, into the language and customs of the sea, and into other subjects of nautical interest.

The Society ensured the survival of Nelson's flagship by raising the Save the *Victory* Fund and has been closely associated with her restoration. It has assisted the Frigate *Foudroyant* in her present role of youth training and, more recently, supported the return of S. S. *Great Britain* from the Falkland Islands and the placing of her in the dock at Bristol from which she was launched in 1843.

The Society paved the way for the foundation of the National Maritime Museum at Greenwich and the new Royal Naval Museum at Portsmouth.

The Society's quarterly journal *The Mariner's Mirror* is internationally recognized as a leading authority in nautical history and archaeology and information about seafaring throughout the ages.

Subscription rates are as follows:

	Commencing 1 January 1986	
	Canada & USA	*All other Countries*
Ordinary Members	$30	£15
Institutional Members	$40	£20

Enquiries relating to the Society and its activities should be made to the Hon. Secretary, The Society for Nautical Research, 2 Drakes Drive, Northwood, Middlesex HA6 2SL.

Also available from Ashford Press Publishing:

Pacific Sail

Four Centuries of European Ships in the Pacific
Text and Paintings by Roger Morris

From Magellan's first voyage, the vast Pacific Ocean has been navigated by numberless sailing ships from Europe. *Pacific Sail* is about these ships and their evolution and of course the men who sailed them, particularly those pioneers of exploration, piracy, war and trade.

Roger Morris has illustrated the whole range of vessels – from the famous names of the *Discovery, Beagle, Endeavour* and *Bounty* to the lesser-known clippers to California, immigrant ships to Australia, and even the humble coastal scows.

Hardback
60 full colour illustrations
ISBN: 1 85253 031 6
September 1987